60 DAYS OF

Happiness

DISCOVER GOD'S PROMISE
OF RELENTLESS JOY

RANDY ALCORN

Tyndale House Publishers, Inc.
Carol Stream, Illinois

Visit Tyndale online at www.tyndale.com.

TYNDALE and Tyndale's quill logo are registered trademarks of Tyndale House Publishers, Inc.

60 Days of Happiness: Discover God's Promise of Relentless Joy

Designed by Jennifer Ghionzoli

Edited by Stephanie Rische

TO CHRIS & JENNY IVESTER,

lovers of Jesus

who show his happiness to the world.

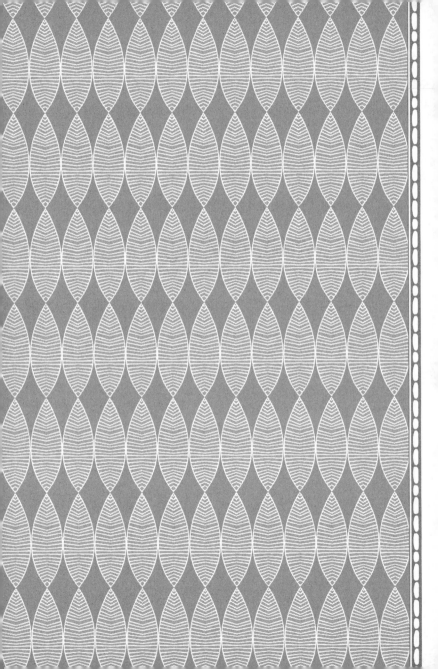

contents

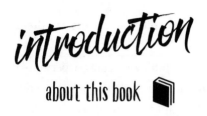

introduction

about this book

WHEN IT COMES TO HAPPINESS, most of us have a lot of questions.

- *Is it possible to be happy when life is much harder than I expected?*
- *Is happiness something people of faith should long for?*
- *Does God even want me to be happy?*
- *And perhaps the most burning questions of all: Why am I not happy, and how in the world can I become happier?*

Over the years, some Christians have made the claim that happiness is unspiritual—that if you want to be holy, then you can't be happy. But that's not true to the Bible or Christian tradition.

Our problem isn't that we want to be happy; our problem is that we keep looking for happiness in all the wrong places. This book will take you to the primary source of happiness in the universe—God. It will then connect the secondary sources of happiness back to the God who created them and graciously gives them to us.

In the process, I think you may experience some paradigm shifts that will bring a smile to your face and forever change your view of happiness and what God thinks of it. It may also change your perspective on God's nature, causing you to see him in a way that floods you with gladness and increases your fondness toward your Creator. I believe you will end up not only loving him more but liking him better. At least, that's what happened to me as I studied Scripture and meditated on this subject for more than three years.

How This Book Came to Be

This book is drawn from carefully selected portions of my larger book *Happiness*. However, I've reworked the material to present it in a fresh and different way. I hope it not only informs you about one of the most appealing subjects in the world but also encourages you, motivates you, and moves your affections toward God.

I've received many encouraging responses to *Happiness*, partly because the subject matter is close to our hearts, whether or not we realize it. But it's not just the subject of happiness that draws people; it's seeing for the first time that God is happy, that he has made us to be happy, and that he has gone to incredible lengths to procure our eternal happiness.

While I've written the big book *Happiness* and also a very small one, *God's Promise of Happiness*, I felt the need for a medium-sized book for those who want more than the one and less than the other.

With the help of an editor and friend, Doreen Button, I selected the subjects I'd researched that most lent themselves to personal growth and worshipful meditation on God and his Word. The Scripture passages, inspirational quotations, and prayers that are part of each meditation help it touch the heart. But the biblical substance and theological implications of these topics will also deepen your mind and broaden your perspective. I hope these truths will delight you and bring insight that will infuse your life with happiness.

The Bible is my go-to source. But I also draw from a number of people who have gone before us in church history—people who faced life and learned lessons we can benefit from.

If you already know Jesus and believe the Bible, you will understand why it's at the center of this book. But if you're not sure, I hope you will continue reading nonetheless and discover God's Word speaking to you in profound and even supernatural ways. (By supernatural, I'm referring to the enlightenment of God's Holy Spirit, who can speak not only to believers but also to unbelievers, by drawing their minds and hearts toward the Good News of Jesus.)

How to Use This Book

This collection of short, self-contained meditations can be used as a standard day-at-a-time devotional. Or you can read it straight through as a conventional book with lots of short chapters, moving on to the next whenever you feel like it, not obliged to wait until the next day. Either approach should work well.

Who This Book Is For

I wrote this for two kinds of readers: first, those who *haven't* read *Happiness* but long to learn what God has to say about this subject and what his people have said about happiness throughout the centuries. It's for anyone who likes to deal with subjects in bite-sized chunks that are also heart-touching and practical.

Second, it's for those who *have* read *Happiness* but would like to return to the subject and ponder it in a devotional format that will likely speak to them in different ways. Some of what they read earlier will be reinforced, but much will feel brand new.

This book is also for those who want to pass on the exciting and paradigm-shifting concepts of *Happiness* but in a smaller and more easily digestible form that may suit their friends or family better.

It wasn't easy to select only sixty snapshots of *Happiness* for these meditations. There's so much more to be said! But I hope and pray these daily readings will help ignite your passion for the happy God and for the gospel of Jesus, which the Bible calls the "good news of happiness" (Isaiah 52:7) and the "good news that will cause great joy" (Luke 2:10, NIV).

If, when you're done, you want a more detailed exploration of this fascinating subject and the many Bible passages that speak of it, you may wish to consult the larger book, *Happiness*. If you want a small pass-along book that's a quick read and shares the happy-making Good News of Jesus, you'll want to consider *God's Promise of Happiness*.

For now, I invite you to join me in meeting the happy God on these pages and the pages of the Bible. Come listen to the Author and Source of happiness. Sit at the feet of him who wired you to want happiness. Consider the invitation of the one who wants you, even in a world full of suffering and struggles, to find in him the happiness each one of us longs for.

Randy Alcorn

-DAY 1-

Why do we all want happiness?

The people the LORD has freed will return and enter Jerusalem with joy. Their happiness will last forever. They will have joy and gladness, and all sadness and sorrow will be gone far away. ISAIAH 51:11, NCV

While other worldviews lead us to sit in the midst of life's joys, foreseeing the coming sorrows, Christianity empowers its people to sit in the midst of this world's sorrows, tasting the coming joy. TIMOTHY KELLER

THE FEVERISH PURSUIT of happiness in our culture might lead us to believe it's a passing fad, the worldview equivalent of bell-bottoms or Beanie Babies. Not so. The desire for happiness isn't, as many suppose, the child of modern self-obsession. The thirst for happiness is deeply embedded in all people, in every culture, and even in God's Word.

The Shawshank Redemption contains a poignant scene in which a prisoner, Andy, locks himself into a restricted area and plays a record featuring opera singers.

1

Beautiful music pours through the public address system while prisoners and guards stare upward, transfixed.

Another prisoner, Red, played by Morgan Freeman, narrates:

I have no idea to this day what those two Italian ladies were singing about. . . . I'd like to think they were singing about something so beautiful, it can't be expressed in words, and makes your heart ache because of it. I tell you, those voices soared higher and farther than anybody in a gray place dares to dream. It was like some beautiful bird flapped into our drab little cage and made those walls dissolve away, and for the briefest of moments, every last man in Shawshank felt free.[1]

The music liberated those prisoners, stirring feelings of a better reality and instilling hope that true beauty exists. We, too, though living in a fallen world, dare to hope for a transcendent happiness that's out there . . . somewhere.

I have fond memories of my childhood and the idealistic dreams of my early life. But by the time I was a teenager, I was disillusioned and empty—though most who knew me wouldn't have guessed.

In junior high I got good grades, won awards, played quarterback, was named team captain, and was elected student body president, but I wasn't happy. I had brief tastes of happiness, but I spent far more time seeking and longing for happiness than experiencing it. I bought comic books by the hundreds, subscribed to fantasy and science fiction magazines, and spent nights gazing through my telescope, pondering the universe, longing for something better.

The night sky filled me with awe—and a small taste of happiness. I yearned for something bigger than myself. (Since I knew nothing of God, aliens were the primary candidates—somehow I knew that this world by itself didn't have enough for me.) One unforgettable night, I gazed at the great galaxy of Andromeda, 2.5 million light-years away, with its trillion stars. I longed to explore it someday, to lose myself in its immensity.

But my wonder was trumped by an unbearable sense of loneliness and separation. I wept that night because I felt so incredibly small. Unknown to me, God was using the marvels of his universe to draw me to himself. Through God's creation, I was seeing "his invisible attributes . . . his eternal power and divine nature" (Romans 1:20).

When I first read the Bible, it was new, intriguing, and utterly disorienting. I opened it and discovered these words: "In the beginning, God created the heavens and the earth" (Genesis 1:1). Then I read the greatest understatement ever: "He made the stars also" (Genesis 1:16, KJV). Countless stars in a universe one hundred billion light-years across are a mere add-on: "also."

I realized that this book was about a person who made the universe, including Andromeda and Earth—and me.

Because I had no reference points when I read the Bible, it wasn't just Leviticus that confused me. But when I reached the Gospels, something changed. I was fascinated by Jesus. Everything about him had the ring of truth, and soon I came to believe he was real. Then, by a miracle of grace, he transformed me—and the single most noticeable difference was my newfound happiness.

My father, angry that I'd turned to a belief he disdained, predicted I would "outgrow" my conversion. I'm grateful that forty-five years later, I haven't. (I'm also grateful that at age eighty-five, four years before his death, my dad trusted Christ.)

Like everyone else, I've experienced suffering and heartaches in my life. Still, every day I find happiness in the one who reached out to me with his grace decades ago—and continues to do so whenever I call out to him. I hope you'll join me in this journey and that together we will experience the life-changing happiness of God.

Lord, we live in a world that sells false happiness at newsstands, stores, and websites. Thank you for offering us authentic happiness in Jesus. Help us to remember that our desire for true happiness comes from you and can only be fulfilled by you, the happy God.

-DAY 2-

What does "being happy in Jesus" mean?

Be happy and full of joy, because the LORD has done a wonderful thing.   JOEL 2:21, NCV

In him the day-spring from on high has visited the world; and happy are we, forever happy, if that day-star arise in our hearts.   MATTHEW HENRY

MOST CHRIST-FOLLOWERS I've known experienced a new-found gladness after their conversions. Sure, life was still difficult, but they had "the peace of God, which surpasses all understanding" (Philippians 4:7). Perhaps that is your story. Or maybe your happiness as a Christian has been reduced to an oasis here and there as you struggle to walk what seems to be an endless desert.

As is the case for many people who are raised in unbelieving homes, the happiness I found in Jesus was a dramatic change.

I first heard about Christ as a teenager, when I visited a church youth group. Initially, Bible stories seemed to me like the Greek mythology and comics I loved. Then I read the Gospels, and I came to believe that Jesus was real and superheroes are his shadows. I felt a profound happiness I'd never known.

My heartfelt gladness was the result of being born again, forgiven, and indwelt by God's Spirit. This happiness stood in stark contrast to the emptiness I'd felt before hearing the gospel's "good news of happiness" (Isaiah 52:7). My parents immediately noticed the change. (Mom liked it; Dad didn't.)

Sure, I needed to make some changes, but I never considered the things I gave up to follow Christ as sacrifices—mainly because they hadn't brought me real happiness. My worst days as a believer seemed better than my best days before knowing Christ. Jesus meant everything to me. I wasn't attempting to be happy; I simply was happy.

Even today, four and a half decades later, I've never forgotten that infectious experience of happiness, which I believe was part of my "first love" for Jesus (Revelation 2:4, NASB). Sometimes regaining that initial passion involves repentance and calling upon God's grace and empowerment. David prayed, "Restore to me the joy of your salvation and grant me a willing spirit, to sustain me" (Psalm 51:12, NIV). He recognized that he couldn't make himself full of joy. Rather, he needed to ask God to restore his gladness and draw his spirit to want to delight in God. I don't think that was a one-time prayer for David—nor should it be for us.

Notice that David, talking to God, called his salvation "your salvation." If we're to discover or rediscover the joy of a relationship with God, we need to start by recognizing that it's centered on what God does, not what we do. We didn't rescue ourselves; God rescued us. So this book isn't about working hard to try to be happy but about asking God to move our hearts to enter into his happiness.

Don't misunderstand. I'm no stranger to unhappiness—in this world under the curse of evil and suffering, something would be wrong if I were. I've studied the Holocaust, walked through the Killing Fields of Cambodia, written at length on persecution and the problem of evil and suffering, and walked alongside people who have experienced profound tragedy and grief. I've experienced illness, adversity, loss, depression, and discouragement. I'm not naturally sanguine, perky, or bubbly. But by God's grace, as the years have passed, I've experienced a more consistent heartfelt gladness and delight in Christ.

True happiness, the kind God wants for us, is not pasting on a false smile in the midst of heartache. It's discovering a reasonable, attainable delight in Christ that transcends difficult circumstances. This desire is obtainable because it's built on God's all-encompassing sovereignty, love, goodness, grace, gladness, and redemptive purposes in our lives.

Until Christ completely cures us and this world, our

happiness will be punctuated by times of great sorrow. But that doesn't mean we can't be predominantly happy in Christ. Our happiness can and should be solidly grounded not on pretense or indifference to suffering or on wishful thinking but on what is absolutely true! It's based on solid facts: God secured our eternal happiness through a cross and an empty tomb, and he grants us lives of purpose, meaning, and eternal significance. He is with us and in us right this moment. He tells us to be happy in him—and he never commands us to do anything without giving us his power to obey.

God, you of all people know how much we crave happiness—you're the one who designed us to crave it! Thank you for giving us both the means and the opportunity to attain it, despite this world's heartaches. Thank you especially for your provision of salvation in Jesus. Remind us daily that by our Savior's redemptive death for us, you've secured for us an eternity free from pain and sorrow, where we'll forever be truly happy. Help us live today in light of that truth.

–DAY 3–

Is happiness unspiritual?

They come with happiness and joy; they enter the king's palace.
PSALM 45:15, NCV

All your security, freedom, rest, peace, and happiness consist in the goodness and love of your Maker towards you.
WILHELMUS À BRAKEL

I'VE WATCHED PEOPLE in several countries view the *JESUS* film for the first time. They beam as Jesus befriends children and performs miracles, groan and weep at his crucifixion, and smile or cry out with delight when they witness his resurrection. The reality of who Jesus is overwhelms them. (I'm told that at one showing, tribal warriors spontaneously jumped to their feet and riddled the screen with blowgun darts in an attempt to stop the soldiers from nailing Jesus to the cross.)

I've also watched videos of tribal groups hearing about eternal life in Jesus for the first time. People repent, turn to Jesus, break out in joyful shouts, and dance for hours.[1]

A video of the Kimyal tribe in Indonesia conveys the over-whelming happiness of those receiving the first Bible in their own language. The occasion, marked by joyful tears, broad smiles, and spontaneous dancing, demonstrates the contagious happiness of people who delight in reading God's words in their heart language.[2]

The Bible is a vast reservoir containing not dozens but hundreds of passages conveying happiness. God says, "My word that goes out from my mouth . . . will not return to me empty, but will accomplish what I desire and achieve the purpose for which I sent it" (Isaiah 55:11, NIV). (That promise is for his words, not mine or yours, which is why this book contains so much Scripture.)

What God says differs radically from what many people— unbelievers and believers alike—assume.

If we don't explore the happiness-related words God put in the Bible, we'll miss the richness of happiness in Christ lying beneath the surface of Scripture. While no treatment of joy and happiness should deny or minimize texts of lamentation, a truly biblical doctrine of joy and happiness fully recognizes and embraces the realities of suffering in this present age. Happiness in Scripture is all the deeper and richer because it doesn't require denial or pretense. We can experience it even in the midst of severe difficulty.

Some argue that the word *happy* is too unspiritual for Christians to use. But those who have studied the Hebrew word *asher* and the Greek word *makarios*, which are frequently used in Scripture, know that those words definitely convey happiness.

Unfortunately, both words are most often translated "blessed" in the most widely read translations (though many other translations render them "happy"). In 1611, when the King James Version was translated, *blessed* was a synonym for *happy*. So whether or not we recognize it, the Bible has talked about being happy all along.

Growing up in an unbelieving home, I never heard the word *blessed*. After I came to Christ I heard the word countless times. I didn't know what it meant; I just knew it sounded holy and spiritual. It was "white noise"—one of many church words whose meanings are masked due to constant use.

Years later, I heard someone say that in passages such as Psalm 1 and the beatitudes of Matthew 5 and Luke 6, *blessed* means "happy." My response was, "Huh?"

Because of what I'd read and been taught, I was certain this must be wrong. In passing years, I've dug for the truth, and my search has yielded rich and surprising discoveries—including that there are more than twenty different Hebrew words and fifteen Greek words in Scripture that are happiness synonyms. The Bible is full of references to happiness.

Despite the original language's meaning, there's a prejudice against using the words *happy* and *happiness* in English Bible translations. About thirty years ago, my friend John R.

Kohlenberger III, the author of dozens of Hebrew and Greek reference books, handed the newly updated New International Version to the religion editor of a major newspaper. She immediately turned to the Beatitudes in Matthew 5 and was relieved to see that it said *blessed*—it passed her test. To her, *blessed* was spiritual and *happy* was unspiritual. Her primary concern didn't seem to be what the original language actually meant but how the English translation sounded.

But *happy* isn't the only word with baggage—many good words are commonly misused and watered down. The word *holy* has lots of baggage too. To countless people, it means being self-righteous, intolerant, and out of touch with reality. Since people routinely misunderstand it, should we avoid the word *holy*? *Love* is commonly used in superficial ways, as popular music has long demonstrated. People say they love hamburgers, hairstyles, and YouTube. They "make love" to someone they barely know. Since the word *love* has been so trivialized, should we remove it from Bible translations and stop using the word in our families and churches?

Of course not. Instead, we should clarify what Scripture actually means by love and holiness, as well as hope, peace, pleasure, and yes, happiness. When appropriate, we should contrast the meaning in Scripture with our culture's superficial and sometimes sinful connotations.

The world and the church once agreed that happiness was good and that all people seek it. We desperately need holiness, but it's happiness we long for, and the church shouldn't retreat from such an important word. On the contrary, we should give it a biblical context, reclaim it, celebrate it, and embrace it as part of the gospel message.

———————

Dear God, you have shown us so clearly that the gospel of your Son is good news because it brings happiness to all who embrace it. Thank you for sending your Word who became flesh—Jesus—and thank you for sending happiness through him.

-DAY 4-

Where did our desire for happiness originate?

Let everything that breathes sing praises to the LORD! Praise the LORD! PSALM 150:6, NLT

It is as natural for the reasonable creature to desire to be happy, as it is for the fire to burn.
THOMAS MANTON

THE FIRST PANEL OF a cartoon shows happy schoolchildren entering a street-level subway station—laughing, playing, tossing their hats in the air. The next panel shows middle-aged adults emerging from the station looking like zombies—dull, joyless, utterly unenthusiastic. A study indicates that children laugh an average of four hundred times daily, adults only fifteen.[1] So what happens between childhood and maturity that diminishes our capacity for happiness?

Based on the books I've read, the sermons I've heard, and the conversations I've had, I'm convinced that many Christians believe our desire for happiness doesn't come from God but was birthed in humankind's fall.

Were we merely the product of natural selection and survival of the fittest, we'd have no grounds for believing any ancient happiness existed. But even those who have never been taught about the Fall and the Curse intuitively know that something is seriously wrong.

Why else would we long for happiness and sense what a utopian society should look like even if we've never seen one? We are nostalgic for an Eden we've only seen hints of. Medieval scholar Anselm of Canterbury (1033–1109) lamented humanity's fall and the loss of the happiness that comes from knowing God: "O wretched lot of man, when he hath lost that for which he was made! . . . He has lost the blessedness [happiness] for which he was made, and has found the misery for which he was not made."[2]

What if Anselm was right and God made us for happiness, and therefore our desire to be happy is inseparable from our longing for God? What if God wired his image bearers for happiness before sin entered the world, and what if that wiring can be properly directed at him and all he wants for us? How might this perspective change our approach to life, parenting, church, ministry, business, sports, entertainment, and everything else?

Anglican bishop J. C. Ryle (1816–1900) wrote, "Happiness is what all mankind want to obtain—the desire for it is deeply planted in the human heart."[3] If this desire is "deeply planted" in our hearts, who planted it? Our answer to that question will dramatically affect the way we see the world. Did Adam and Eve want to be happy before they sinned? Did they enjoy the food God provided because it tasted sweet? Did they sit in the sun because it felt warm and jump into the water because it felt refreshing? If we believe God is happy, then doesn't it stand to reason that he would create us with the desire and capacity to be happy?

Yet today, Christ-followers say things like, "God wants you blessed, not happy";[4] "God doesn't want you to be happy. God wants you to be holy";[5] and "God doesn't want you to be happy, he wants you to be strong."[6] But does the message that God doesn't want us to be happy promote the "good news of happiness" spoken of in Isaiah 52:7? Does it reflect the gladness-saturated gospel of redemption in Christ? Or does such antihappiness language obscure the Good News? If happiness is what you want and God doesn't want you to be happy, wouldn't that actually be bad news?

When we separate God from happiness and from our longing for happiness, we undermine the Christian worldview. We might as well say, "Stop breathing and eating; instead, worship God." People must breathe and eat, and they must also desire happiness—and they can worship God as they do so!

Where did our desire for happiness originate?

Lord Jesus, help us to remember, with our every breath, what a precious gift life is. We can't live without you—you are our provider, our protector, and our best friend. Thank you that, regardless of all claims to the contrary, you really do want us to be happy in you. Thanks for not only giving us a desire for happiness but also giving us so many ways we can please you by pursuing happiness in you.

Can happiness be consistent and enduring?

Happy is he who does not condemn himself in what he approves. ROMANS 14:22, NASB

There is no man upon the earth who isn't earnestly seeking after happiness, and it appears abundantly by the variety of ways they so vigorously seek it; they will twist and turn every way, ply all instruments, to make themselves happy men.
JONATHAN EDWARDS

IN *THE SECRET*, Rhonda Byrne tells about Colin, a ten-year-old boy who was dismayed by long waits for rides at Disney World. He'd seen *The Secret* movie, so he focused on the thought that tomorrow he wouldn't have to wait in line. What happened? Colin's family was chosen to be Epcot's "First Family" for the day, putting them first in every line.[1]

Now, we should be grateful when God sends us fun surprises, and had I been part of Colin's family, I'd have been thankful too. But it's one thing to be happy when such things occur and another to expect, demand, or lay claim to them. Our models should be people such as Amy Carmichael (1867–1951), who brought the gospel to countless children she rescued from temple prostitution in India. She experienced a great deal of physical suffering and never had a furlough in her fifty-five years as a missionary. Yet she wrote, "There is nothing dreary and doubtful about [life]. It is meant to be continually joyful. . . . We are called to a settled happiness in the Lord whose joy is our strength."[2]

God makes this settled happiness possible despite life's difficulties. Rich and durable, this happiness is ours today because Christ is here; it's ours tomorrow because Christ will be there; and it's ours forever because he will never leave us.

God's kind of happiness is not a superficial "don't worry, be happy" philosophy that ignores human suffering. The day hasn't yet come when God will "wipe away every tear from [his children's] eyes" (Revelation 21:4). But it will come. And this reality has breathtaking implications for our present happiness.

For many people, happiness comes and goes, changing with the winds of circumstance. Such happiness isn't solid or grounded. We can't count on it tomorrow, much less forever.

We say to ourselves, *I'll be happy when* . . . Yet either we don't get what we want and are unhappy, or we do get what we want and are still unhappy.

Sometimes happiness eludes us because we demand perfection in an imperfect world. It's the Goldilocks syndrome: everything must be "just right," or we're unhappy. And nothing is ever just right! So we don't enjoy the ordinary days that are a little, quite a bit, or even mostly right.

Sometimes we miss out on happiness because we fail to recognize it when it comes or because we fail to contemplate and treasure it. Some people are only happy when they're unhappy. If they have nothing to complain about, they don't know what to do with themselves. But habitual unhappiness is a pitiful way to live. And it doesn't just hurt the unhappy person; it hurts those around him or her, since both happiness and unhappiness are contagious. (Have you ever been to churches you'd describe as unhappy and others that are happy?)

Our happiness will remain unstable until we realize our status in light of eternity. The truth is—and the Bible makes it clear—this life is temporary, but we'll live endlessly somewhere, in a place that's either far better or far worse than this one.

We can find lasting and settled happiness by saying yes to the God who created and redeemed us and by embracing a biblical worldview. When we look at the world and at our daily lives through the lens of redemption, reasons for happiness abound. And while these reasons are at times obscured, they remain permanent.

Father, give us eyes to see all the treasures you've bestowed on us today. Help us to meditate on the deep and abiding happiness that is ours in Christ. Give us patience and faith to wait for the day when you will surpass our wildest dreams and there will be no sin to kill the joy that can only be found in you.

What is true happiness based on?

May all those who seek you be happy and rejoice in you!
PSALM 40:16, NET

*Those who are "beloved of the Lord" must be the most happy
and joyful people to be found anywhere upon the face of
the earth.*   CHARLES SPURGEON

AS CHRISTIANS, our happiness makes the gospel conta-
giously appealing; our unhappiness makes it alarmingly
unattractive. So is the church today known for its happiness
or unhappiness?

Webster's Dictionary defines happiness as—wait for it . . .
"the state of being happy."[1] Synonyms include *pleasure, contentment, satisfaction, cheerfulness, merriment, gaiety, joy,
joyfulness, joviality, delight, good spirits, lightheartedness,* and
well-being.[2]

The *Dictionary of Bible Themes* gives a more biblical

definition of happiness: "A state of pleasure or joy experienced both by people and by God. . . . True happiness derives from a secure and settled knowledge of God and a rejoicing in his works and covenant faithfulness."[3]

Among Christ-followers, happiness was once a positive, desirable word. Only in recent times have happiness and joy been set in contrast with each other. This isn't just biblically and historically ungrounded; it has undermined our understanding of merriment, pleasure, and joy.

Are laughter, celebration, and happiness God-created gifts, or are they ambushes from Satan and our sin nature that incur God's disapproval? Our answer determines whether our faith in God is dragged forward by duty or propelled by delight.

My best times with my wife, Nanci, and our family and friends are filled with Christ-centered interaction and heartfelt laughter. These two experiences aren't at odds but are intertwined. The God we love is the enemy of sin and the creator and friend of fun and laughter.

Many Christians in church history knew that happiness, gladness, feasting, and partying are God's gifts. Can these good things be warped, selfish, superficial, and sinful? Of course. In a fallen world, what can't be?

Believers and unbelievers alike recognize that there's a negative form of happiness, which is all about self-gratification at others' expense. The philosophy "do whatever makes you happy" gets considerable press, but people who live that way end up pathetic and despised.

Is there selfish and superficial happiness? Sure. There's also selfish and superficial love, peace, loyalty, and trust. We shouldn't throw out Christ-centered happiness with the bathwater of self-centered happiness.

Although the quest to be happy isn't new, people today seem to be particularly thirsty for happiness. Our culture is characterized by increasing depression and anxiety, particularly among the young.[4] Studies show that more people feel bad than good after using social media; photos and updates of everyone else having a great time leave observers feeling left out—like they don't measure up.

Numerous Christians live in daily sadness, anger, anxiety, or loneliness, thinking these feelings are inevitable given their circumstances. They lose joy over traffic jams, a line at the grocery store, or increased gas prices. They read Scripture with blinders on, missing the reasons for happiness expressed on nearly every page.

The truth is this: it's impossible to be truly happy, and remain happy, without believing in the sovereignty of a loving God. The beauty of the Christian worldview is that while we're encouraged to take initiative and control what's within our power, we also know that the huge part of life we can't control is under God's governance. Scripture tells us, "Our God is in the heavens; he does all that he pleases" (Psalm 115:3).

It assures us, "The heart of man plans his way, but the LORD establishes his steps" (Proverbs 16:9). And since God is eternally wise and good, and we're not, we're far better off with him in control than if we were. All the circumstances we can't control rest in his hands.

In our fallen world, troubles and challenges are constants. Happy people look beyond their circumstances to Someone so big that by his grace, even great difficulties become manageable—and provide opportunities for a deeper kind of happiness.

Lord Jesus, help us to flee from counterfeit happiness and instead look to you, who have always been and always will be happy. We want to be like you, finding happiness in what makes our Father happy. May we not rely on our circumstances to provide the happiness we long for, but instead fix our eyes on you, the source of all joy.

How can we be happy in such a sad world?

Come to Me, all who are weary and heavy-laden, and I will give you rest. Take My yoke upon you and learn from Me, for I am gentle and humble in heart, and YOU WILL FIND REST FOR YOUR SOULS. For My yoke is easy and My burden is light.
JESUS (MATTHEW 11:28-30, NASB)

The child of God is, from necessity, a joyful man. His sins are forgiven, his soul is justified, his person is adopted, his trials are blessings, his conflicts are victories, his death is immortality, his future is a heaven of inconceivable, unthought-of, untold, and endless blessedness—with such a God, such a Saviour, and such a hope, is he not, ought he not, to be a joyful man? OCTAVIUS WINSLOW

GOD'S LAWS ARE often seen as burdensome, but everything changes when we realize he intended them to secure our happiness. When the gospel is viewed primarily as laying burdens and obligations on people, the Good News gets buried. Burdens

and obligations are not good news; good news is about liberation, deliverance, newfound delight, and celebration. Sure, duty is real and the gospel calls us to a life of obedience, but it's glad duty and joyful obedience.

Consider Christ's example. He said, "My food is to do the will of him who sent me and to accomplish his work" (John 4:34). Food not only keeps us alive; it brings us pleasure. What is Christ's food, his source of happiness? To accomplish his Father's will. Doing and obeying the will of his Father is a delight, not a burden, to Jesus—even though the Cross was the greatest burden in the history of the cosmos, one that makes all other burdens seem insignificant in comparison.

Carrying "light burdens" doesn't mean that bad and demanding things won't happen to us; it means that Jesus will lessen their weight upon us as we trust him and rely upon him to carry the load. Following Christ is to be characterized by "casting all your care on Him, because He cares about you" (1 Peter 5:7, HCSB). This is why Paul could call both his and our considerable sufferings "light and momentary troubles" (2 Corinthians 4:17, NIV).

When we seek holiness at the expense of happiness or happiness at the expense of holiness, we lose both the joy of being holy and the happiness birthed by obedience. God commands holiness, knowing that when we follow his plan, we'll be happy. He also commands happiness, which makes obeying him not only duty but also pleasure.

Sadly, many Christians live as if their faith has drained their happiness! But the same Jesus who calls for sacrifice, promising that we'll share in his suffering, also tells us to lay our burdens at his feet. We're to take up our crosses daily, yet he promises that his burden is light. Life isn't easy, but believers have the benefit of walking the hard roads side by side with a loving Father, a Son who is our friend, and a comforting Holy Spirit.

Paul J. Wadell, in an ethics textbook, says, "Augustine and Aquinas . . . recognized that . . . the heart of the Christian moral life is learning about happiness."[1]

How much better might people respond to Christian ethics if its principles weren't portrayed as burdensome obligations to the God of holiness we fear but as a privilege and a delight in the God of happiness we love?

If holiness and happiness are inseparable, why not do what many churches have done for centuries and appeal to people only on the basis of holiness? Because, though holiness is a deep need of the soul, it's not always a felt need. By God's grace, we can use the desire for happiness to lead people to the holiness that's woven into the gospel with happiness.

Thomas Watson (1620–1686), a Puritan preacher and author, said, "He has no design upon us, but to make us happy. . . . Who should be cheerful, if not the people of God?"[2]

Did you catch that? A Puritan was saying that God's design is to make us happy! What did Watson realize that we don't?

Father, sometimes it's too easy to focus on how tough life is and forget the good things you have filled our world with. You've lightened our burdens by giving us access to your throne of grace, where we're free to unload all our burdens and worries. Thank you—a thousand times over, thank you! May we always remember that following your ways and seeking holiness in you is the greatest happiness there is.

-DAY 8-

Does God want us to be happy or holy?

In the world you will have tribulation; but be of good cheer,
I have overcome the world.   JESUS (JOHN 16:33, NKJV)

Not everyone who has the will for happiness has happiness.
ANSELM

THE FRENCH PHILOSOPHER and mathematician Blaise
Pascal (1623–1662) famously said, "All men seek happiness."
He also wrote these words in his collection of thoughts on
theology:

> *What else does this longing and helplessness*
> *proclaim, but that there was once in each person a*
> *true happiness, of which all that now remains is the*
> *empty print and trace? We try to fill this in vain with*
> *everything around us, seeking in things that are not*
> *there the help we cannot find in those that are there.*

> *Yet none can change things, because this infinite abyss*
> *can only be filled with something that is infinite and*
> *unchanging—in other words, by God himself. God alone*
> *is our true good.*[1]

The Fall didn't generate the human longing for happiness—
it derailed and misdirected it.

Scripture portrays our connection to the sin of Adam in a
way that transcends time—as if we were there in Eden with him
(see Romans 5:12-21). Similarly, I believe we inherited from our
Eden-dwelling ancestors a sense of their pre-Fall happiness.
This explains why our hearts refuse to settle for sin and suffering and we long for something better.

The devil's lie from the beginning was that God doesn't care
about our good. The truth is, God wants us to seek real happiness in him, while Satan wants us to seek false happiness
that will only leave us empty and broken. (There is also false
holiness—the Pharisees had a passionate desire to be holy on
their own terms, resulting in self-congratulatory pride. We
don't invalidate true holiness because of its false forms, and
neither should we invalidate true happiness because many
seek happiness in sin.)

Satan hates God, he hates us, and he hates happiness as
much as he hates holiness—God's and ours. He isn't happy and
has no happiness to give, so he dispenses rat poison in bright,
colorful, happy-looking wrappers. The devil has no power to

implant in us a desire for happiness. Satan is not about happiness; he is about sin and misery, which come from seeking happiness where it can't be found. God is the one who planted our desire for happiness—the devil can't remove it, he can only misdirect it.

Adam and Eve fell away from God and happiness because of their disobedience. However, they never lost their desire to be happy. As their descendants, we inherited their separation from God, and therefore from happiness. Ages later, we retain a profound awareness that we were once happy—and that we should be happy.

This compelling desire for genuine happiness, while at times painful, is God's grace to us. Longing for the happiness humankind once knew, we can be drawn toward true happiness in Christ, which is offered to us in the gospel.

Because we were made for greatness, the world's superficiality is unsatisfying. We sense that unhappiness is abnormal, and we ache for someone, somehow, to bring us lasting happiness. That someone is Jesus, and the somehow is his redemptive work.

When I was a teenager, God used my persistent desire for happiness to prepare me for the gospel message. The "good news of happiness" in Christ (Isaiah 52:7) was exactly the cool water my thirsty young soul craved.

The gospel is good news only to those who know they need

it. Had I been happy without Jesus, I never would have turned to him.

Yet while I heard much about God's holiness at church, Bible college, and seminary, not once did I hear about God's happiness. I have no doubt it would have been surprising, memorable, and encouraging. What better explanation for the flood of happiness that overwhelmed my life after coming to Christ than that my God, who created, redeemed, and indwelt me, was happy?

Though I studied the Bible regularly, somehow the hundreds of Scriptures indicating God's pleasure, delight, and joy didn't register. They were nullified by unbiblical statements I heard from pastors and authors, such as "God calls us to holiness, not happiness."

I've always been a voracious reader, inhaling books, including theological works, by the hundreds. But I didn't read anything about the happiness of God until the late 1980s, after I'd been a pastor for ten years. John Piper's then-new books *Desiring God* and *The Pleasures of God* introduced me to a subject I should have heard about in my first few months attending church as a teenager.

Fortunately, it's never too late to learn. If this book is your first introduction to the idea that God is happy and has wired us to crave happiness in him, I hope it excites and inspires you to realize that your yearning for happiness is a gift from God and that he alone can ultimately satisfy you.

God, we're so grateful that you implanted this intense craving for happiness in us so we would continue searching until we found its source in you. Thank you for providing the way to experience the true happiness you intended for us before the Fall. Help us to never be content with the world's cheap imitations of happiness but to always seek the happiness that's in you and from you.

What do homesickness and happiness have in common?

Happy are the people who know the joyful shout; Yahweh, they walk in the light of Your presence. PSALM 89:15, HCSB

Give me an explanation, first, of the towering eccentricity of man among the brutes; second, of the vast human tradition of some ancient happiness. G. K. CHESTERTON

PSYCHOTHERAPIST LYNNE ROSEN and motivational speaker John Littig cohosted an hour-long radio show on WBAI in New York called *The Pursuit of Happiness*. But this Brooklyn couple's final act was putting plastic bags over each other's heads and committing suicide.[1]

Rosen and Littig were experts in promoting and pursuing happiness yet failures in finding it. This tragic couple epitomizes the irony that the more we advertise and purchase products, events, and books intended to make us happy, the unhappier we may become.

In 1997, thirty-nine members of the cult Heaven's Gate, led by Marshall Applewhite, participated in a mass suicide. They'd been taught that once they exited their earthly bodies, they would land on a spaceship following the Hale-Bopp comet. At the time of their death, each member carried a five-dollar bill and three quarters. Why? To pay an interplanetary toll.

We may shake our heads in amazement at this kind of gullibility. Yet we fail to see the futility of our own misguided attempts to find happiness. Many people try the age-old practices of turning to money, sex, power, beauty, sports, nature, music, art, alcohol, drugs, education, work, or celebrity for happiness. In the end, each of these proves as big a lie as a spaceship on a comet's tail.[2]

The problem for the Heaven's Gate followers wasn't that they trusted too much; it was that they trusted the wrong person. Only Jesus was worthy of their trust. Only he could have granted them, in this life and for eternity, the deep and lasting happiness they sought.

Aren't we all weary of the onslaught of politicians, psychologists, physicians, religious leaders, diet plans, and TV commercials promising more than they can deliver? We have our expectations raised only to be crushed time and time again. Yet we continue to hope for better things, for greater happiness than life's track record suggests is possible.

A. A. Milne (1882–1956), creator of Winnie the Pooh, conveyed the joy of anticipation:

*"Well," said Pooh, "what I like best—" and then he had
to stop and think. Because although Eating Honey was
a very good thing to do, there was a moment just before
you began to eat it which was better than when you
were, but he didn't know what it was called.*[3]

C. S. Lewis (1898–1963) called this anticipation *Sehnsucht*,
a German word for "yearning."[4] Sehnsucht is used to describe
a longing for a far-off country that's, for now at least, unreach-
able. Lewis connected the yearning itself and the foretastes of
it with the joy that is longed for.

Before the Fall, Adam and Eve undoubtedly anticipated good
food, but instead of falling short of expectations, the food in Eden
likely tasted better than imagined. After the Fall, however, the
opposite is true. We expect something more of food, entertainment, and relationships, which are all secondary things compared
to primary happiness in God, and we are inevitably disappointed.
Though we live in a fallen world, we still retain the expectations
and hopes of a better one. Our discontent is healthy, provided it
leads us to look to God for what can't be found elsewhere.

In *The Discarded Image*, C. S. Lewis references a vivid
simile in Chaucer's "The Knight's Tale." The knight describes
the human journey this way: "All men know that the true good
is Happiness, and all men seek it, but, for the most part, by
wrong routes—like a drunk man who knows he has a house
but can't find his way home."[5]

The human race is homesick for Eden, which only two humans have ever known. We know intuitively that we've wandered. What we don't know is how to return. We spend our lives chasing delight, following dead ends or cul-de-sacs in our attempts to get home to Happiness with a capital H—God himself.

A. W. Tozer (1897–1963) wrote, "For whatever else the Fall may have been, it was most certainly a sharp change in man's relation to his Creator. He . . . destroyed the proper Creator-creature relation in which, unknown to him, his true happiness lay."[6]

The quest for happiness transcends gender, age, and life circumstances. Holocaust victim Anne Frank (1929–1945) wrote as a teenager, "We all live with the objective of being happy; our lives are all different and yet the same."[7]

In an 1898 article arguing against religion, L. K. Washburn said, "There is a constant mental pilgrimage towards that Mecca of the human heart—happiness. . . . Everybody wants to be happy, and thinks, strives, wishes, and lives to that end."[8]

How many subjects do Puritans, philosophers, atheists, and agnostics categorically agree on? One of the few is our innate longing for happiness.

Lord, since we were made in your image, we want to be happy as you are happy. Help us look for, and find, happiness only in the things that please you and that we

can enjoy together with you. Thank you that you alone
can satisfy the deepest longings of our hearts and that you
graciously and regularly use secondary things to bring us
happiness from you, the primary source of happiness.

-DAY 10-

Is it possible to separate happiness from God?

All the days of the afflicted are evil, but the cheerful of heart has a continual feast. PROVERBS 15:15

Man was not originally made to mourn; he was made to rejoice. The Garden of Eden was his place of happy abode, and as long as he continued in obedience to God, nothing grew in that Garden that could cause him sorrow. CHARLES SPURGEON

HUMAN HISTORY IS the story of our desperate search for true and lasting happiness. Even those people who seem to "have it all" long for something more, often quietly giving up hope of ever finding real joy.

Psychiatrist Paul D. Meier writes,

I have had millionaire businessmen come to my office and tell me they have big houses, yachts, condominiums . . . , nice children, a beautiful

mistress, an unsuspecting wife, secure corporate positions—and suicidal tendencies. They have everything this world has to offer except one thing— inner peace and joy. They come to my office as a last resort, begging me to help them conquer the urge to kill themselves.[1]

In the midst of such hopelessness, God offers the good news of his transforming grace, mercy, love, and eternal happiness: "Let the one who is thirsty come; let the one who wants it take the water of life free of charge" (Revelation 22:17, NET).

Charles Darwin (1809–1882), near the end of his life, spoke of what he called his "loss of happiness":

Up to the age of thirty, or beyond it, poetry of many kinds . . . gave me great pleasure, and even as a schoolboy I took intense delight in Shakespeare. . . . Formerly pictures gave me considerable, and music very great delight. But now for many years I cannot endure to read a line of poetry: I have tried lately to read Shakespeare, and found it so intolerably dull that it nauseated me. . . . My mind seems to have become a kind of machine for grinding general laws out of large collections of facts. . . . The loss of these tastes is a loss of happiness.[2]

Darwin may not have traced his diminished happiness to his gradual change in worldview, but it's likely that the naturalistic perspective he embraced gradually undermined his early delight in studying God's creation, resulting in a joyless, machinelike indifference.

Thomas Traherne (1636–1674), an English poet and theologian, wrote, "Till you can sing and rejoice and delight in God . . . you never enjoy the world."[3]

Yes, unbelievers can experience limited joy, but when we know and love the Creator, our heartfelt delight is magnified. Seeking happiness without God is like seeking water without wetness or sun without light.

In an 1847 letter to his father, Scottish author George Macdonald (1824–1905) wrote of the barriers he faced in turning to Christ:

One of my greatest difficulties in consenting to think of religion was that I thought I should have to give up my beautiful thoughts & my love for the things God has made. But I find that the happiness springing from all things not in themselves sinful is much increased by religion. God is the God of the Beautiful, Religion the Love of the Beautiful, & Heaven the House of the Beautiful—nature is tenfold brighter in the sun of righteousness, and my love of nature is more intense since I became a Christian. . . . God has not given me

*such thoughts, & forbidden me to enjoy them. Will he
not in them enable me to raise the voice of praise?*[4]

Loving nature and beauty should indeed be enhanced by
loving the God who made them and reveals himself in them—
how could it be otherwise?

Living in Oregon, surrounded by stunning natural beauty
and people who love and sometimes worship it, I often ponder the irony that my state and our neighbor, Washington,
have among the lowest percentages of Christ-followers
anywhere in the United States. According to a Gallup poll,
Portland, Oregon, where Nanci and I and our children were
born, is tied with Seattle and San Francisco for the highest percentage of "religiously unaffiliated" people in the
United States.[5]

So if happiness comes from God, does this mean people
who live in Portland can't be happy? No, because for the present, by God's grace and kindness, people can reject God but
still enjoy the benefits of his common grace, including loving
relationships, natural and artistic beauty, and physical, emotional, and intellectual pleasure.

The bad news is that those who deny God are living on bor-
rowed time. This temporary situation will come to an abrupt
end (see Hebrews 9:27-28; Revelation 20:11-15).

After the termination of this life, we can have one of two
combinations:

1. both God and happiness
2. neither God nor happiness

What we won't be able to have is God without happiness or happiness without God.

Father, thank you for your common grace that allows everyone to enjoy the beauty of your creation. Thank you for your saving grace that allows us to see you as the one to whom those beauties testify. Thank you for your patience and mercy that allow us time and motivation in this life to seek you and experience your happiness.

What's the difference between joy and happiness?

The godly are happy; they rejoice before God and are overcome with joy.   PSALM 68:3, NET

No man in the world should be so happy as a man of God. It is one continual source of gladness.   DWIGHT L. MOODY

A HUNDRED YEARS AGO, every Christian knew the meaning of joy. Today, if you ask a group of Christians, "What does joy mean?" most will grope for words, with only one emphatic response: that joy is different from happiness. It's supposedly superior—deep rather than superficial, holy rather than sinful. It's often said to be unemotional, in contrast to that unspiritual thing called happiness. (This also sends the message that anything emotional is bad.)

Saying that joy isn't about being happy is like saying that rain isn't wet or ice isn't cold. Scripture, church history, dictionaries, and common language simply don't support this conclusion.

I googled "define joy," and the first result was this dictionary definition: "a feeling of great pleasure and happiness." This definition harmonizes with other dictionaries and ordinary conversations, yet it contradicts countless Christian books and sermons that claim joy and happiness are radically different.

The church's misguided distinction between joy and happiness has twisted the words. A Christian psychiatrist says, "Happiness is secular, joy sacred."[1] So we should be joyful but not happy when reading the Bible, praying, and worshiping? Is the Christian life really divided into the secular and sacred, or is every part of our lives, even the ordinary moments, to be centered in God?

God created not only our minds but also our hearts. Sure, emotions can be manipulated, but so can minds. God designed us to have emotions, and he doesn't want us to shun or disregard them. It's ill advised to redefine joy and happiness and pit them against each other rather than embracing the emotional satisfaction of knowing, loving, and following Jesus.

I've become so accustomed to reading misstatements by contemporary Christians about joy and happiness that when I read a devotional by Joni Eareckson Tada I cheered aloud at her words. Tada opens by citing Psalm 68:3: "May the righteous be glad and rejoice before God; may they be happy and joyful" (NIV). She then writes:

We're often taught to be careful of the difference between joy and happiness. Happiness, it is said, is an emotion that depends upon what "happens." Joy by contrast, is supposed to be enduring, stemming deep from within our soul and which is not affected by the circumstances surrounding us. . . . I don't think God had any such hair-splitting in mind. Scripture uses the terms interchangeably along with words like delight, gladness, blessed. There is no scale of relative spiritual values applied to any of these. Happiness is not relegated to fleshly-minded sinners nor joy to heaven-bound saints.[2]

Joni Eareckson Tada is absolutely right. Modern distinctions between happiness and joy are completely counterintuitive. This is no minor semantic issue. For too long we've distanced the gospel from what Augustine, Aquinas, Pascal, the Puritans, Wesley, Moody, and many other spiritual visionaries said God created us to desire—and what he desires for us—happiness.

Do we seriously want to take issue with Charles Spurgeon (1834–1892) when he said, "My dear Brothers and Sisters, if anybody in the world ought to be happy, we are the people. . . . How boundless our privileges! How brilliant our hopes!"[3] Was he wrong to say we ought to be happy, and would his meaning be more spiritual if he'd said "joyful" instead? To declare joy sacred and happiness secular closes the door to dialogue with unbelievers.

If we say the gospel won't bring happiness, any perceptive listener should respond, "Then how is this gospel good news?" If the gospel we believe doesn't make us happy, then it is certainly not what Scripture calls the "good news of happiness" (Isaiah 52:7).

We need to reverse the trend. Let's redeem the word *happiness* in light of both Scripture and church history. Our message shouldn't be "Don't seek happiness" but "You'll find in Jesus the happiness you've always longed for."

Lord, we are so easily confused. Please fill us so full of your truth that we can see through false distinctions made by sincere spiritual leaders who teach something you never said and restate it as if it were your inspired Word. We've done the same thing, Lord, and we need your guidance to think biblically and accurately. Help us to rejoice, be happy, be glad, and take delight in you, and remind us that it's impossible to do one of those things without doing all of them!

If happiness isn't joy, what is?

Shout triumphantly to the LORD, all the earth! Be happy! Rejoice out loud!   PSALM 98:4, CEB

The devil cannot bear to see one of Christ's people happy, so he tries constantly to disturb their joy.   A. W. PINK

IT'S NEEDLESS, distracting, and misleading to make fine distinctions between joy, happiness, gladness, merriment, and delight. They all speak with one voice of a heart experiencing the goodness of God and his countless gifts.

Yet most of us have encountered books, articles, and sermons telling us that joy is spiritual and happiness is secular,[1] that happiness is an emotion dependent on circumstances,[2] that joy is not an emotion but a choice,[3] that joy is the opposite of happiness,[4] and that happiness is fleeting and temporal while joy is eternal.[5] You'll see articles and sermons with titles such as "Happiness Is Not Joy"[6] and "Happiness Is the Enemy of Joy."[7] And despite hundreds of biblical statements that suggest otherwise, you'll hear, "There is absolutely nothing in the Bible that says that God wants you to be happy."[8]

So why have so many Christ-followers come to speak so negatively about happiness? Perhaps since physical delights may be involved, we are suspicious that someone who is happy must be sinning. If that's the case, what does that say about our worldview?

Perhaps we marginalize happiness because something inside us testifies that we—who were snatched from the jaws of Hell to Heaven's eternal delights, who are indwelt and empowered by a happy God—should really be happier than we are. Maybe by reducing joy to something unemotional, positional, or transcendental—or even inhuman—we can justify our unhappiness, in spite of God's command to rejoice always in him. Maybe saying that joy doesn't involve happiness allows us to lower the bar and accept a more downtrodden, cheerless Christian life.

Throughout the 1987 movie *The Princess Bride*, the Sicilian mastermind Vizzini repeatedly uses the word *inconceivable* to describe event after event that actually happens. Finally, Inigo Montoya tells Vizzini, "You keep using that word. I do not think it means what you think it means."

This statement also applies to that frequently used but terribly misunderstood word *joy*. It doesn't mean what many people think and say it means: something unemotional. It means something far richer and better: delight, pleasure, and emotional satisfaction. It means happiness.

Speaking to unbelievers, Paul said of God, "He did not leave Himself without a witness, since He did what is good by giving you rain from heaven and fruitful seasons and satisfying your hearts with food and happiness" (Acts 14:17, HCSB). Eight translations render the Greek word "happiness," fourteen others use "joy," and more than twenty others say "gladness." Any and all of these translations are correct since happiness, joy, and gladness are close synonyms. Note also that these terms are applicable to believers and unbelievers alike. By God's grace, believers can know happiness and unbelievers can experience joy. Paul was building a bridge to the gospel through identifying God as the universal source of happiness. Until recent times, the idea of happiness has been a bridge between the church and world, between the gospel and unbelievers—and it's a bridge we can't afford to burn.

However, there's a significant difference between the happiness of believers and unbelievers. First, the happiness of the unconverted is limited to the present. King David spoke of people whose reward is in this life (see Psalm 17:14). Abraham spoke to the rich man in Hell, saying, "Remember that in your lifetime you received your good things" (Luke 16:25, NET).

Second, the happiness of this life enjoyed by the unconverted is largely dependent on favorable circumstances (see Psalm 73:18-19; Matthew 19:22). In light of Scripture's call to joy, delight, gladness, and happiness in God, we need to abandon the idea that we can't be happy in a sin-stained culture and that it's unspiritual to be cheerful in a hurting world. God's Word says otherwise.

Do we really wish to distance the gospel and the church from happiness? If we succeed, we'll distance them from the world, too, for the world will go right on wanting happiness. Christians shouldn't abandon happiness—we should embrace the true, holy, heartwarming, and beautiful happiness Scripture freely offers through God's persistent and everlasting love.

Lord, we can't be happy without your presence in us—at least not for long. Help us use the gifts you've so freely given to draw closer to you and to demonstrate in our little worlds the delight you poured into the whole universe when you first made it. Thank you that you haven't given up on that world, just as you haven't given up on us. Thank you that you don't eliminate our emotions but redeem them. When life is tough, remind us of all we have to be thankful for, and fill our hearts with your supernatural happiness as we contemplate our joy-filled eternity to come.

Is happiness the world's imitation of joy?

You, O LORD, have made me happy by your work. I will sing for joy because of what you have done.   PSALM 92:4, NET

If you have nice little categories for "joy is what Christians have" and "happiness is what the world has," you can scrap those when you go to the Bible, because the Bible is indiscriminate in its uses of the language of happiness and joy and contentment and satisfaction.   JOHN PIPER

WHILE RESEARCHING and writing my book *Happiness*, I had dozens of nearly identical conversations.

Someone asked, "What are you writing about?"

I responded, "Happiness."

Unbelievers were immediately interested. Believers typically gave me an odd look, as if to say, "Don't you usually write on spiritual themes?" They often responded, "You said *happiness*—did you mean *joy*?"

A pastor friend wrote to tell me why it would be a big mistake to write a book about happiness. He said what he'd been taught to think: "Happiness changes from moment to moment and is reflected by our moods and emotions. Joy is a spiritual peace and contentment that only comes from God and is strong even during times of sadness. God's desire is not to make us happy in this life but to fill our lives with joy as a result of our relationship with Christ."

My first pastor often cited *My Utmost for His Highest* by Oswald Chambers (1874–1917), and I eagerly read that great book as a young Christian. But at the time I didn't know enough to disagree with this statement: "Joy should not be confused with happiness. In fact, it is an insult to Jesus Christ to use the word happiness in connection with Him."[1] I certainly didn't want to insult Jesus, so after reading this and many similar statements in books and sermons, I became wary of happiness.

Many people I've talked with have the distinct impression that Scripture distinguishes between joy and happiness. They think the Bible depicts all joy as godly and all happiness as ungodly.

A book on Christian ministry has a chapter called "Happiness vs. Joy." It says, "Joy and happiness are very different."[2]

In a chapter titled "Joy versus Happiness" another Christian author states, "Happiness is a feeling, while joy is a state of being."[3]

Another claims, "Joy is distinctly a Christian word and a Christian thing. It is the reverse of happiness."[4]

In an article called "Jesus Doesn't Want You to Be Happy," the author states, "As you read through the gospels you'll see plenty of promises of joy, but none of happiness. And they are infinitely different things."[5]

Happiness is the *reverse* of joy? The two are *infinitely different*? Really? What is the scriptural, historical, or linguistic basis for making such statements? There simply is none! Is there nothing more to joy than "a state of being"? Is emotion something we should reject, or is it a gift of God, part of being made in his likeness?

Since these emphatic proclamations against happiness are so common, and since they're spoken by those who believe the Bible, it seems to most Christians that they must be right. But when I was a young Christian, they made me uneasy, because before reading such things and hearing them from the pulpit, I had celebrated my newfound happiness in Christ. Now I was being told that happiness was at the very least suspect and dangerous, and even unspiritual, and had no place in a serious Christian life.

To me, this was counterintuitive. Of course, I knew we shouldn't turn to sin for happiness—or anything else—but happiness was something I gained when I came to Christ, not something I gave up!

If it was God who made me happy to be forgiven and gave me the joy of a right relationship with him, was God really against my happiness?

I didn't yet realize that Scripture said, "Happy are those

55

whose sins are forgiven, whose wrongs are pardoned" (Psalm 32:1, GNT). And "How happy is the man who takes refuge in Him!" (Psalm 34:8, HCSB). I read those passages but only in a version that said "blessed" instead of "happy." So I had no clue what those passages really meant. If I had, my soul would have resonated because they state exactly what I had found in Jesus!

Joy is a perfectly good word, and I use it frequently. But there are other equally good words with overlapping meanings, including *happiness*, *gladness*, *merriment*, *delight*, and *pleasure*. Depicting joy in contrast with happiness has obscured the true meaning of both words. After conducting a thorough study of the Bible's original languages, I'm convinced this is an artificial distinction.

Joyful people are typically glad and cheerful—they smile and laugh a lot. To put it plainly, they're happy! God cares about our happiness, and we should too.

Father, deliver us from the widespread notions that rob both happiness and joy of their biblical and historical richness. Please help us radiate such happiness that those who don't yet know you want to experience that same joy for themselves. We're so thankful to be loved by you. Empower us to demonstrate an authentic spirit of delighted gratitude to everyone around us.

-DAY 14-

Is God happy?

God . . . in eternal felicity alone holds sway. He is King of kings and Lord of lords. 1 TIMOTHY 6:15, NEB

Where others see but the dawn coming over the hill, I see the soul of God shouting for joy. WILLIAM BLAKE

WHAT ACCOUNTS FOR Christians not experiencing the happiness and joy the Bible so often speaks of? I'm convinced a central reason—perhaps the central reason—is that many people who believe in God do not believe that God himself is happy. And how could anyone expect that knowing and serving an unhappy God would bring us happiness?

In the movie *Chariots of Fire*, Olympic hopeful and eventual gold medalist Eric Liddell is challenged by his sister, Jennie, about his decision to train for the Olympics. He plans to leave for the mission field but delays so he can attempt to qualify in the 400-meter race. In doing so, Jennie thinks he's putting God second. But Eric sees things differently.

He explains, "God . . . made me fast, and when I run I feel his pleasure."[1]

Eric and Jennie believe in the same God . . . yet they don't. Both fear and love God. Both are committed to serving Christ. But Eric, who smiles warmly and signs autographs while his sister looks on disapprovingly, has something she lacks: a relaxed, heartfelt awareness of God's happiness—in his creation, in his people, and in all of life, including sports and competition.

Eric wants to serve God as much as his sister does, but he senses God's delight and purpose in making him a fast runner. If God finds pleasure in the majesty of a horse (see Job 39:19-25), surely he finds even greater pleasure in Eric's running for the pure joy of it. Because of the God-centered joy this gift brings him, Eric tells Jennie that giving up running "would be to hold [God] in contempt."[2]

Both Eric and his sister want to reach the world with the gospel. But Eric's good news is far better news. Why? Because it's about more than deliverance from Hell—he understands that God's mind and heart are delightfully engaged in all he has created, not just church and ministry. Liddell's belief in a happy God makes his life profoundly attractive.

When we think of God as happy, we see how his happiness overflows in all he does. If your grumpy neighbor asks, "What are you up to?" you'll see it as a suspicious, condemning question. But if your cheerful neighbor asks the same thing, you'll smile and talk about your plans. We interpret people's words according to how we perceive their character and outlook. So it is with our view of God.

If we think God is unhappy, we will interpret his words in Scripture accordingly. When he tells us not to do certain things, we'll think he's trying to keep us from happiness. But if we know God to be happy, we will understand that he tells us to avoid things because, like a loving parent who tells a child to stay away from the highway, he wants us to be safe and happy.

To be godly is to resemble God. If God is unhappy, we'd need to pursue unhappiness, which is as likely as developing an appetite for gravel. If following Jesus means having to turn away from happiness, and we're wired to want happiness, then we can only fail as Christians. The wonderful news is that when we look at Scripture carefully, we find a happy God who desires us to draw happiness from him. Yet how many Christians have ever heard a sermon, read a book, had a discussion about, or meditated on God's happiness?

You may be thinking, *But does the Bible really say God is happy?* The answer is yes—it does! Many times Scripture states that God experiences delight and pleasure. Other times when it affirms God's happiness, readers of English Bibles don't understand what the original language was communicating.

The apostle Paul wrote of "the gospel of the glory of the blessed [*makarios*] God with which I have been entrusted" (1 Timothy 1:11). Later in the same book, he refers to God as "he who is the blessed [*makarios*] and only Sovereign, the King of kings and Lord of lords" (6:15). In 1611, when King James translators chose the word *blessed* in verses like these, it meant "happy"! In fact, the 1828 edition of Noah Webster's dictionary still defined *blessed* as, "Made happy or prosperous; extolled; pronounced happy. . . . Happy . . . enjoying spiritual happiness and the favor of God; enjoying heavenly felicity."[3]

Likewise, Webster defined *blessedly* as "happily" and *blessedness* as "happiness." So, two hundred years after the KJV was translated, people still understood *blessed* to mean "happy."

In contrast, a poll I did of more than one thousand people, mostly Christians, indicated that only 12 percent of them associate *blessed* with *happy*. Most others think of *blessed* not as a happiness word but as a holiness word. Hence, while "blessed" was a good translation four hundred years ago and still good two hundred years ago, it is no longer a good translation, because it fails to convey the happiness connotations of the original word. The fact is that 1 Timothy 1:11 and 6:15 actually speak of the gospel of the "happy God" and the God "who is the happy and only Sovereign."

I'm convinced that in the new universe—called in Scripture the New Heaven and the New Earth—the attribute of God's happiness will be apparent everywhere. Upon their deaths, Christ-followers won't hear, "Go and submit to your master's harshness" but "Come and share your master's happiness!"

(Matthew 25:21, NIV). Anticipating those amazing words can sustain us through every heartbreak and challenge in our present lives.

———

Father, thank you that you have revealed yourself to us in your Word as the happy God. Jesus, thank you for being our example of God's triune happiness. You loved and laughed and lived—and still do—as the Son with whom the Father is well pleased. Help us grow up to be just like you!

-DAY 15-

How does understanding God's happiness change lives?

Behold, I create new heavens and a new earth. . . . Be glad and rejoice forever in that which I create; for behold, I create Jerusalem to be a joy, and her people to be a gladness. I will rejoice in Jerusalem and be glad in my people; no more shall be heard in it the sound of weeping and the cry of distress.

ISAIAH 65:17-19

What comes into our minds when we think about God is the most important thing about us. A. W. TOZER

A TEENAGE BOY CAME to me with questions about his faith. He'd attended church all his life but now had some doubts. I assured him that even the writers of the Bible sometimes struggled. He wasn't questioning any basic Christian beliefs, and he didn't need six evidences for Christ's resurrection, so I talked to him about holiness and happiness.

"What does God's holiness mean?" I asked.

His clear, biblical answer: "He's perfect, without sin."

"Absolutely true. Does thinking about God's holiness draw you to him?"

He responded sadly, "No."

I asked him whether he wanted to be holy 100 percent of the time. "No."

"Me neither. I should, but I don't."

Then I surprised him, asking, "What do you want 100 percent of the time?" He didn't know.

"Have you ever once thought, *I don't want to be happy*?"

"No."

"Isn't that what you really want—happiness?"

He nodded, his expression saying, "Guilty as charged." Friendships, video games, sports, academics—every activity, every relationship he chose—played into his desire to be happy. But I could see he felt that this longing was unspiritual, displeasing to God.

I told him the word translated "blessed" in 1 Timothy 1:11 and 6:15 speaks of God being happy. I asked him to memorize these verses, replacing "blessed God" with "happy God."

Then I asked him to list whatever pointed him to God's happiness—backpacking, music, playing hockey, favorite foods. I said, "God could have made food without flavor, but he's a happy God, so he created a world full of happiness. That means you can thank him for macaroni and cheese, for music, for Ping-Pong, and above all, for dying on the cross so you can know him and be forever happy."

This boy had seen Christianity as a list of things he should do that wouldn't make him happy and a list of things he shouldn't do that would have made him happy.

Since we'll inevitably seek what we believe will bring us happiness, what subject is more important than the true source of happiness? Just as we'll live a wealth-centered life if we believe wealth brings happiness, so we'll live a God-centered life if we believe God will bring us happiness. No one shops for milk at an auto parts store or seeks happiness from a cranky God.

As much as I believe in the holiness of God, I also believe in emphasizing God's happiness as a legitimate and effective way to share the gospel with unbelievers or to help Christians regain a foothold in their faith.

God feels love, compassion, anger, and happiness. He's never overwhelmed by unsettling emotions, nor is he subject to distresses imposed by others. But he does feel his children's suffering deeply.

If your human father said he loved you but never showed it through his emotions, would you believe him? If we think God has no emotions, it's impossible to believe he delights in us or to feel his love. That's one reason believing in God's happiness can be a breakthrough for people in their love for him.

We're told of God, in relationship with his people, "In all their affliction he was afflicted. . . . In his love and in his pity he redeemed them; he lifted them up and carried them all the days of old" (Isaiah 63:9). What a moving portrayal of the tenderness of his affection for us and devotion to us!

But if God is so moved by our sorrows, how can he still be happy while we're suffering?

God himself models his inspired command to rejoice always. He sympathizes with all his suffering children, but he rejoices in purchasing our redemption and making us more like Jesus. He joyfully prepares a place for us, and he has eternally happy plans. He has the power to accomplish everything, as well as the sure knowledge that it will happen.

While I'm grateful that God cares deeply for me, I'm also grateful that when I'm miserable, it doesn't mean God is. As any good father will be moved by his daughter's pain when her boyfriend breaks up with her, God can feel our pain while retaining his own happiness. God the Father has an infinitely larger picture of eventual, eternal good that he will certainly accomplish. Nothing is outside his control. Therefore, nothing is a cause for worry. God does not fret.

Yes, our distress can involve feelings God doesn't have, such as helplessness or uncertainty. But clearly God intends for us to see a similarity between our emotional distress and the affliction he feels on our behalf. If God experiences various nonsinful human emotions, as indicated by Scripture, it stands to reason that he feels happiness, too.

———

Loving Father, you are all-knowing, so nothing takes you by surprise. You are all-powerful, so there's nothing you want to do but can't. You are completely loving and good, so you can never and will never betray or abandon us. You are the source of all happiness, so you're able to fulfill our deepest longings for joy and pleasure. Thank you for being both capable of and committed to bringing ultimate goodness to us, your children.

-DAY 16-

What is God's promise for our future happiness?

Sing, Jerusalem. Israel, shout for joy! Jerusalem, be happy and rejoice with all your heart.   ZEPHANIAH 3:14, NCV

I arrive where . . . the more complete the soul the more happy its joys, where is full knowledge of thee.
THE VALLEY OF VISION: A COLLECTION OF PURITAN
PRAYERS AND DEVOTIONS

IN MY NOVEL *SAFELY HOME*, I tell the story of two Harvard roommates reunited in China twenty years after graduation. One is American businessman Ben Fielding, an entrepreneur in international high-tech corporate partnerships. The other is Li Quan, a brilliant academic who, when Ben last saw him, was headed home to be a professor at a Chinese university.

When Ben reconnects with Li Quan on a business trip to China, he's shocked to find his old friend living in poverty, working as a locksmith's assistant, and involved with a house church often raided by the police. Shortly after the two become reacquainted, Quan is imprisoned. Yet even in prison, to Ben's astonishment, Quan remains cheerful, trusting God and rejoicing in his goodness despite enduring cruel treatment.

The longer Ben stays in China and the more time he spends with Li Quan and his wife and son, the more he envies his old friend. Even with everything he has going for him and everything working against Quan, Ben realizes he wishes he could trade places with his former roommate. Why? Because Quan has what Ben doesn't: love and happiness. Li Quan drew his happiness from God, who was with him even in prison. Ben Fielding attempted to find happiness in everything the world had to offer . . . and failed miserably.

Central to Li Quan's happiness, and that of millions of believers who have endured suffering, is the recognition that this world, as it now is, is not their home. Therefore they should not let their faith rest on their country, government, circumstances, health, and wealth. Rather, they know that God has made them citizens of another country. One day he will bring about a New Earth, which he will rule forever with justice and love.

This is why Peter says to suffering believers in this world gone wrong, "But we wait for what God has promised: new heavens and a new earth, where righteousness will be at home" (2 Peter 3:13, GNT).

World peace and universal happiness seem like utopian

dreams, but these dreams are not far fetched, because according to God's Word, utopia once existed and will again. (What's far fetched is believing we are capable of creating this utopia ourselves!)

It should delight us to hear that the future involves a return to Paradise. Jesus promised his disciples that one day there will be a "renewal of all things" (Matthew 19:28, NIV), which the English Standard Version translates as "the new world" and the Complete Jewish Bible renders as "the regenerated world."

Just as we'll take on our eternal, resurrected bodies, the world itself will be resurrected. Peter preached that Christ would not return "until the time for restoring all the things about which God spoke by the mouth of his holy prophets long ago" (Acts 3:21). The New Century Version translates this as "when all things will be made right again." Our entire experience on the New Earth will be of happiness far greater than Adam and Eve could have ever imagined!

The past will be remembered as that temporary period of rebellion when God's creatures turned from him. We'll celebrate endlessly that Jesus entered our history to redeem us and to restore the shared happiness of God and his people.

The apostle John, aided by an angel, time-traveled to the New Earth. There he saw "the water of life, as clear as crystal, flowing from the throne of God and of the Lamb down the middle of the great street of the city. On each side of the river stood the tree of life." He went on to explain what life will be like for those who live in the New Earth: "No longer will there be any curse. The throne of God and of the Lamb will be in the city, and his servants will serve him. They will see his face" (Revelation 22:1-4, NIV).

As God's children, we have a history of his faithfulness in the past and an assurance of a secure future, which should define how we view our present. This perspective can infuse us with happiness even in what would otherwise be the unhappiest times of our lives.

God so wants us to be happy that he plans to re-create the universe, raise us from the dead, and give us back the wonders of Eden multiplied a thousand times over. There we'll live in joyful, never-ending communion with him, all bought and paid for with his own blood.

Seriously . . . could anything we might invent or imagine begin to compare with what God has promised and secured for us, the children he loves?

Lord Jesus, we don't deserve anything you've done for us, much less all of it. Your grace truly is amazing. Thank you for redeeming us and preparing a paradise for us to share with you and each other forever. Help us to live each day anticipating what lies ahead and experiencing a foretaste of the boundless happiness that awaits us.

-DAY 17-

Does obeying God mean sacrificing our happiness?

Until now you have asked nothing in my name. Ask, and you will receive, that your joy may be full. JESUS (JOHN 16:24)

It is a Christian duty . . . for everyone to be as happy as he can.
C. S. LEWIS

YOU MAY BE UNACCUSTOMED TO thinking that God commands us to be happy or to do things that make us happy. But he does. And I'd wager that since the outcome of our obedience would be our happiness, these are commands we would all want to obey—provided we were thinking clearly.

Some people have an intuitive resistance to the notion that happiness is unbiblical, and rightfully so. A blogger says, "Happiness isn't in the Bible? But what about all the commands to rejoice? What about laughter? Please tell me I'm not supposed to always be heavy-hearted, trudging along and begrudging obedience. I want to be a happy Christian!"[1]

Happiness is a privilege. However, since God repeatedly calls upon us to rejoice, delight, and be glad in him, we have an obligation to actually do so.

This makes sense only if the God we love is happy, if the gospel message we embrace and proclaim is happy, if Heaven is a happy place, and if it makes God happy for us to be happy. It makes sense if we understand that people long to be happy and won't turn to Jesus if they believe there's no happiness in him.

Others will judge whether there's happiness in Jesus by whether they see happiness in his followers. Hence, our happiness is, in multiple respects, a Christian duty.

But what an incredibly wonderful duty it is . . . like being required to eat Mom's apple pie! We're accustomed to thinking of duty as drudgery. Yet we know that the duties of loving a spouse or caring for a child or serving one's country can bring satisfaction, contentment, and happiness.

People have told me it's easy to speak of happiness in a prosperous country, but how dare we say God expects those impoverished and suffering to be joyful? In fact, poor Christians often have joy that radiates far beyond what we typically see in Western churches, and they have much to teach us.

I've studied more than 2,700 Scripture passages where words such as *joy, happiness, gladness, merriment, pleasure, celebration, cheer, laughter, delight, jubilation, feasting, exultation,* and *celebration* are used. Throw in the words *blessed* and *blessing,* which often connote happiness, and the number increases.

Even Jeremiah, who's called "the weeping prophet" since he was brokenhearted over the tragic suffering of God's people, spoke prophecies of happiness. He saw the future—some of it in this world's Jerusalem and much of it in the New Jerusalem to come—and in it he was given glimpses of God's promised happiness.

God is clear that seeking happiness—or joy, gladness, delight, or pleasure—through sin is wrong and fruitless. But seeking happiness in him is good and right.

So should we feel guilty for being unhappy, struggling with depression, and being sad at the suffering in our lives and others' lives? No, but we should feel a liberating hope that Jesus, who knows infinitely more about suffering than we do, offers us and calls us to greater happiness than we've known.

As Jeremiah and Jesus wept, we, too, will sometimes weep—and so we should. But if we're not experiencing some degree of happiness in God, then we're not obeying God's commands and we're missing out on the abundant life Jesus came to give us (see John 10:10).

Let's say yes to his offered gift of happiness in him. Your temperament may be like mine—not naturally joyful, but more melancholic and prone to depression. You may not become the happiest person you know, but just as I have, you, too, can become far happier in Christ than you ever could have on your own.

Over the years, as I have contemplated Scripture, walked

with God, and sought to cultivate an eternal perspective, my happiness has increased. None of us are prisoners of our natural temperaments. We too quickly underestimate the Holy Spirit's power to transform us gradually into the image of Christ (see 2 Corinthians 3:18).

The fruit of the Spirit described in Galatians 5:22-23, including joy, is the Holy Spirit doing a supernatural work in our lives. What we cannot do in ourselves he can do in us when we yield ourselves to him.

I talked with a young woman who viewed the Christian life as one of utter dullness. She knew that following Christ was the right thing to do, but she was certain it would mean sacrificing her happiness.

Unless her view changes dramatically, her spiritual future is bleak. It isn't in our nature to continually say no to what we believe would make us happy—or to say yes to something we think would make us unhappy. (Don't mistake perseverance for choosing unhappiness—the man who faithfully loves his wife suffering from dementia is not choosing unhappiness but rather choosing the happiness of honoring his wife, keeping his vows, maintaining his self-respect, and hearing God's "well done.")

So where did this young woman, who was raised in a fine Christian family and church, acquire such an unbiblical notion? Somehow she, like many of us, missed the point of what God calls the good news of great joy.

Around 150 years ago, Pastor Charles Spurgeon told his church what pastors today should tell theirs: "God made human beings, as He made His other creatures, to be happy. . . . They are in their right element when they are happy."[2]

Celebration and gladness of heart have characterized the church, including the suffering church, throughout history. Scripturally, the culture of God's people is not one of misery, anger, and whining but of joy, happiness, gratitude, eating and drinking, singing and dancing, and making music. It's not the people who know God who have reason to be miserable—it's those who don't.

What a wonderful God *you are to not only provide a means of happiness but also to command us to be happy even as you command us to be holy. How happy we should be to love and be loved by someone as delightful as you! Thank you for creating us so that our happiness increases as our gratitude multiplies. This is joy unspeakable. We praise you for calling us to ever-greater happiness in you, your presence, your Word, your creation, and your work in our lives and in the world around us.*

-DAY 18-

Why aren't Christians known for their happiness?

We all, who with unveiled faces contemplate the Lord's glory, are being transformed into his image with ever-increasing glory, which comes from the Lord, who is the Spirit.

2 CORINTHIANS 3:18, NIV

Let us leave sadness to the devil and his angels. As for us, what can we be but rejoicing and glad? FRANCIS OF ASSISI

WHEN OUR FACE TO the world is one of anger, misery, shame, cowardice, or defensiveness, the gospel we speak of doesn't appear to be the good news of happiness. And we shouldn't be surprised if people, both outside and inside the church, aren't attracted to it. Why should they be?

Children who grow up seeing church as a morose, hyper-critical place will turn their backs on it in their quest for happiness. Those who have found happiness in the church will usually stay or return.

Sadly, many non-Christian young adults today view Christ's followers as "hypocritical," "insensitive," and "judgmental."[1] These words all describe unhappy people. (If the world judges us, so be it, but it shouldn't be because we're chronically unhappy.)

I see two extremes of Christians when it comes to happiness. Some immediately change the channel from the coverage of a hurricane, refuse to acknowledge sex trafficking and abortion, and ignore the sufferings of this world while grabbing on to superficial living. They look the other way when their marriages are in trouble or when their children choose wrong friends, because they don't want to see or admit anything that might require empathy or hard work. They hold fast to their false notion that denying problems buys them happiness.

Other Christians are perpetually somber, never laughing or poking fun at themselves, rarely celebrating, and quick to frown when they see someone having fun. Shoulders sagging, they believe that happiness is ungodliness, and their calling in life is to be the one who doesn't laugh at the joke. (Granted, there are some jokes the holy person should never laugh at, but the truly holy person will be a happy person, quick to laugh at humor that doesn't dishonor God.)

Paul said he was "sorrowful, yet always rejoicing" (2 Corinthians 6:10). Sorrow and joy can and do coexist, for now. (Note that the "always" in this verse is applied to rejoicing, not being sorrowful. This means our lives should be characterized more by joy than by sorrow.)

If we constantly focus on all that's wrong with the world, then sorrow or anger will be our default. But the apostle Paul, writing from prison in Rome, called on his fellow believers to rejoice in the Lord not periodically, but always (see Philippians 4:4). You rejoice not simply by reflecting on the fact that you should but by actually choosing to set your mind on what brings joy—Jesus and his love, the beauties of the world God has created, the daily kindnesses of God, the gifts and providential divine appointments he brings to us, people around us who help us, material provisions, food and drink and the ability to enjoy them, and a thousand other things in and around and over us.

When Puritan Jonathan Edwards (1703-1758) was only nineteen years old, he made a resolution that speaks volumes: "Resolved, to endeavor to obtain for myself as much happiness in the other world as I possibly can, with all the power, might, vigour, and vehemence . . . I am capable of."[2]

In the movie *The Stepford Wives*, husbands program "perfect" wives. Of course, these robotic wives are perfect only in the sense that they do whatever their husbands want. But what any good man really desires is a relationship with a real person who responds out of heartfelt love and happiness. Fake, programmed love or happiness is empty—in fact, it's unreal. God doesn't force happiness on us, nor does he call us to pretend we're happy when we're not. Rather, he invites us to enter his happiness and find it in him.

Parents repeat instructions to children because kids tend

to miss it the first time. Hence Paul said, "Again I will say, rejoice" (Philippians 4:4). He wanted to make sure we'd get it. Synonyms for happiness appear repeatedly throughout Scripture. If God says it enough, shouldn't we get it? Still, most of us have failed to notice the cumulative force of the biblical revelation that we are to be consistently happy in God.

It's not insensitive, unkind, or wrong for us to be happy! By being happy in Christ, we lay claim to the fact that God is bigger than the Fall and affirm that our Lord and Savior Jesus Christ indwells us and will reverse the Curse and reign over a new universe. Our happiness shouts that our God is present with us and at work in the world every minute of every hour of every day. The narrower our view of God's presence in this world—and in our daily lives—the less happiness we'll experience.

———

Lord Jesus, you've told us repeatedly in your Word that we're to be happy in you. When we are, we know it makes you happy. Help us remember our countless reasons for happiness and to share that good news with the world. Enable us to delight you and others with kind acts and cheerful words, which offer the bonus of delighting us, too.

–DAY 19–

Must we choose between our happiness and God's glory?

All the people of Judah were happy because they had made this covenant with all their heart. They took delight in worshiping the LORD, and he accepted them and gave them peace on every side. 2 CHRONICLES 15:15, GNT

I assert without hesitation, that the conversion described in Scripture is a happy thing and not a miserable one, and that if converted persons are not happy, the fault must be in themselves.... I am confident the converted man is the happiest man. J. C. RYLE

CHRISTOPHER PARKENING, considered by many to be the world's greatest classical guitarist, achieved his musical dreams by the age of thirty. By then he was also a world-class fly-fishing champion.

However, success failed to bring him happiness. Weary of performances and recording sessions, Parkening bought a ranch and gave up on the guitar. But instead of finding happiness after getting away from it all, his life became increasingly empty. He wrote, "If you arrive at a point in your life where you have everything that you've ever wanted and thought would make you happy and it still doesn't, then you start questioning things. It's the pot of gold at the end of the rainbow. I had that and I thought, 'Well, what's left?'"

While visiting friends, Parkening attended church and put his faith in Christ. He developed a hunger for Scripture and was struck by 1 Corinthians 10:31: "Whatever you do, do it all for the glory of God" (NIV).

He explains, "I realized there were only two things I knew how to do: fly fish for trout and play the guitar. Well, I am playing the guitar today absolutely by the grace of God. . . . I have a joy, a peace, and a deep-down fulfillment in my life I never had before. My life has purpose. . . . I've learned first-hand the true secret of genuine happiness."[1]

Charles Spurgeon also loved to connect the gospel and happiness: "There is nothing that more tends to strengthen the faith of the young believer than to hear the veteran Christian, covered with scars from the battle, testifying that the service of his Master is a happy service, and that, if he could have served any other master, he would not have done so, for His service is pleasant, and His reward everlasting joy."[2]

If we weigh the value of our happiness against the needs of a suffering world, we may suppose we have no right to be happy. But the fact is, unhappy Christians have little to offer a suffering world. Our happiness in Christ, which involves not indifference but heartfelt compassion, allows us to help others and share with them the joy in Christ. It is this same happiness that energizes and sustains us as we serve God and others.

Of course, if we compare the value of our happiness to the value of God and his glory, our happiness is far outweighed. But the same is true of everything else. God and his glory are infinitely more important than our families, friendships, churches, and jobs, but that doesn't mean any of those people and things are unimportant. Indeed, God himself tells us they are important.

Such a comparison also makes the false assumption that God's glory and our happiness fall on two different sides of a balance, to be weighed against each other. On the contrary, they are inextricably linked—both are parts of his design and plan. God is glorified when we are happy in him, so our happiness shouldn't be weighed against his glory but seen as part of it.

A. W. Tozer wrote, "The people of God ought to be the happiest people in all the wide world! People should be coming to us constantly and asking the source of our joy and delight."[3] Tozer's statement is grounded on the belief that God is happy. This is what makes our happiness in God both possible and significant. Not first and foremost because we want to be happy (though of course we do), but because *God* made us to want to be happy and because he himself truly wants us to be happy.

If people are not coming to us and asking us the source of our joy and delight, it should cause us to reflect on our view of God's happiness. We should ask him to empower us to delight in him more for his glory, our good, and the good of those around us who desperately need to see and hear the "good news of great joy" in Jesus (Luke 2:10).

————

Jesus, you gave your life so we could be together forever, experiencing true happiness and delight. Help us share your delight so that our friends and family and neighbors see in us your gladness and are eagerly drawn to join in your joy and ours. May we remember that being happy in you brings you the greatest glory.

If Christians shouldn't be happy, who should be?

You will fill me with joy when I am with you. You will make me happy forever at your right hand. PSALM 16:11, NIrV

Affirming that by transgression of God's commandments [Adam and Eve] might attain to felicity and joy . . . [the devil] caused them to seek life where God had pronounced death to be.
JOHN KNOX

G. K. CHESTERTON (1874–1936) has been widely credited with saying, "Jesus promised His disciples three things—that they would be completely fearless, absurdly happy, and in constant trouble." It might be argued that most Western Christians aren't any of these three—least of all "absurdly happy."

Christianity is perceived to be about tradition and morality, not happiness. I've taught college courses on biblical ethics, and I make no apologies for believing in morality. But some Christians, in the name of moral obligation, go around with frowns on their faces, dutifully living a paint-by-numbers religious existence and proudly refraining from what "lesser" people do to be happy. They seem to wear their displeasure as a badge of honor.

Ironically, the church has given unbelievers reason to fear that becoming a Christian will result in their unhappiness. They've known—as many of us churchgoers have also known—professing Christians who go out of their way to promote misery, not gladness. I've seen Bible-believing, Christ-centered people post thoughts on a blog or on social media only to receive a string of outraged responses from people who wield Scripture verses like pickaxes, swiftly condemning the slightest hint of a viewpoint they consider suspicious. If I were an unbeliever reading such responses, I certainly wouldn't be drawn to the Christian faith.

I wonder why it's not immediately recognized by those engaging in such behavior that what they're doing is utterly contrary to the faith they profess and the Bible they believe. How is it that perpetual disdain, suspicion, unkindness, and hostility are seen as taking the spiritual high ground? Perhaps the message that Christians shouldn't be happy has really been taken to heart!

Curmudgeonly Christianity abounds. Some professing Christians feel morally superior to those who engage with culture, and as a result, they major on making world-condemning judgments. They proudly abstain from laughter. They assume that barbecues and ball games are the spawn of sin. Grim-faced pharisaical "Christians" make Satan's propaganda campaign far easier by undermining the Good News and promoting a negative view of happiness.

Who would ever be drawn to the worldview of decidedly unhappy people? Consider satirist and journalist H. L. Mencken's (1880–1956) definition of Puritanism: "the haunting fear that someone, somewhere, may be happy."[1] (On the contrary, Puritans, judging by their writings, were some of the happiest people who have ever lived! Considerably happier, judging by his writings, than H. L. Mencken.)

In most unbelievers' perceptions, Christianity hasn't brought much joy to the world. As a religion, it's primarily known for its rules, self-righteousness, and intolerance—none of which convey gladness and merriment.

This is not the whole story, of course. Throughout history, the Christian worldview has accounted for happiness-generating developments such as hospitals and schools, science and industry, music, drama, and the arts. And on a more personal level, nearly every community includes people with quiet confidence in Christ who are extraordinarily loving, kind, helpful, and cheerful. They gladly give of their time and money to those in need. Such people are rarely in the public eye, but they certainly exist. Sadly, however, to many people, they seem to be the exception rather than the rule.

Thomas Aquinas (1225–1274) wrote, "Man is unable not to

wish to be happy."[2] This means that all attempts by Christians to disregard or demean happiness are misguided and unfruitful. By creating distance between the gospel and happiness, we send the unbiblical (and historically ungrounded) message that the Christian faith is dull and dreary.

Let's speak against sin but hold up Christ as the happiness everyone longs for. If we don't, then we will assure our own unhappiness and feed the world's perception that Christianity takes away happiness instead of bringing it.

Holy Spirit, please remove from me anything that would turn someone away from you. Please fill me so full of yourself that your happiness spills over onto everyone I meet today. Thank you that in your presence there is fullness of joy. And whenever I lack that joy, please draw me back to your presence for a refill.

Are humankind's desires sinful?

You are the LORD's people! So celebrate and praise the only God. PSALM 97:12, CEV

Christ [is] the very essence of all delights and pleasures, the very soul and substance of them. As all the rivers are gathered into the ocean . . . so Christ is that ocean in which all true delights and pleasures meet. JOHN FLAVEL

C. S. LEWIS WROTE,

> *If there lurks in most modern minds the notion that to desire our own good and earnestly to hope for the enjoyment of it is a bad thing, I submit that this notion . . . is no part of the Christian faith. Indeed, if we consider the unblushing promises of reward and the staggering nature of the rewards promised in the Gospels, it would seem that Our Lord finds our desires, not too strong, but too weak. We are*

half-hearted creatures, fooling about with drink and
sex and ambition when infinite joy is offered us, like an
ignorant child who wants to go on making mud pies in
a slum because he cannot imagine what is meant by
the offer of a holiday at the sea. We are far too easily
pleased.[1]

When I first read these words, having known Christ for only a few years, it was paradigm shifting. In my brief church experience, I'd learned many wonderful things, but I'd also been taught that God was opposed to our pursuit of happiness. When I delighted in something "secular," such as music or science fiction or a good movie, I felt vaguely guilty, as if my pleasure displeased God.

But Lewis had a different perspective. He wasn't saying that alcohol, sex, and ambition were inherently wrong, only that God—who created these things—deserves the highest place in our hearts. While we can enjoy the gifts God has given us in the appropriate time and place, they'll never be able to give us the deep happiness and satisfaction we find in him. Finding our greatest pleasure in God elevates our enjoyment of those happiness-giving things. They're transformed from mud pies to mouthwatering desserts to be fully enjoyed at the celebratory table of God's goodness.

When I was a young Christian, one of the hymns often sung at my church featured these words:

Turn your eyes upon Jesus,
Look full in his wonderful face,
And the things of earth will grow strangely dim,
In the light of his glory and grace.[2]

Unless "things of earth" mean only that which is sinful, these words don't make sense. Shouldn't drawing close to our Creator make the beauties and wonders of his Earth brighter to us, not dimmer? Instead of turning away from the Earth's wonders in order to see God, shouldn't we be able to see God in them?

After coming to Christ, Jonathan Edwards commented on that very topic:

The appearance of everything was altered; there
seemed to be, as it were, a calm, sweet cast or
appearance of divine glory in almost everything. God's
excellency, his wisdom, his purity and love, seemed to
appear in everything; in the sun, moon, and stars; in
the clouds and blue sky; in the grass, flowers, trees; in
the water and all nature.[3]

For Edwards, his conversion caused him to love God's creation more, not less. As I've walked with God over the years, the sin-centered and shallow attractions of this Earth have indeed grown dimmer, but the happy-making beauty of this

Earth's animals, trees, flowers, oceans, and sky, and of friends, family, good stories, music, and food have grown brighter.

Thomas Aquinas, the most influential theologian of the Middle Ages, said, "No one can live without delight, and that is why a man deprived of spiritual joy goes over to carnal pleasures."[4] We crave joy, delight, pleasure—in a word: happiness.

Being happy in God and living righteously tastes far better for far longer than sin does. When my hunger and thirst for joy is satisfied by Christ, sin becomes unattractive. I say no to sin not because I hate pleasure but because I want the greatest and most enduring pleasures found in Christ.

———

Lord, you want us to give you everything—heart, mind, and body. You know that our only hope for lasting happiness lies in giving up what we can't keep anyway in order to gain that which never fades, rusts, or withers. Please help us desire you more than anything and anyone else. May we see following you not as turning away from pleasure but pursuing the best and most enduring pleasure.

-DAY 22-

What's so good about the Good News?

I bring you good news of great joy that will be for all the people.
AN ANGEL OF THE LORD (LUKE 2:10)

The religion of Christ is the religion of JOY. Christ came to take
away our sins, to roll off our curse, to unbind our chains, to
open our prison-house, to cancel our debt. . . . Is not this joy?
Where can we find a joy so real, so deep, so pure, so lasting?
There is every element of joy—deep, ecstatic, satisfying,
sanctifying joy—in the gospel of Christ. The believer in Jesus
is essentially a happy man.   OCTAVIUS WINSLOW

THE ANGEL'S MESSAGE TO the shepherds at the birth of
Jesus condenses the gospel to its core: the "good news of great
joy" wasn't for some; it was "for all the people." This is truly
the best news there has ever been or ever will be.

What characterizes this good news is a deep, everlasting
joy for any who will receive it. The Contemporary English

Version renders Luke 2:10 this way: "good news for you, which will make everyone happy."

The world Jesus entered desperately needed a redeemer from sin, hopelessness, and unhappiness. The mythological Greek gods (which the Romans had renamed) were seldom taken seriously. In daily life, Greek and Roman worldviews were centered more on Stoicism or Epicureanism, both of which failed to bring happiness.[1]

The Stoics believed in truth and virtue. They exercised mental disciplines that allowed them to overcome emotions and rise above difficulties, similar to some forms of Buddhism today. Scholar William Morrice states, "There was no joy in it. Stoicism was essentially pessimistic in spirit, and its outlook upon life was dark and foreboding."[2]

Epicureanism, on the other hand, taught that happiness was found in enjoying life's pleasures. According to Epicurus, "There was no place at all in religion for joy—except in the case of the gods themselves, who lived a life of perpetual happiness and bliss. The self-appointed task of the philosopher was to free men from the terrors and degradations of religion."[3]

Stoicism and Epicureanism have close counterparts in contemporary Western culture. As a religion, modern Christianity is viewed, sometimes unfairly and sometimes not, much like Stoicism: a duty-driven, negative, unhappy way of life.

The secular backlash against Christianity today has much in common with Epicureanism. Its message is to be happy however and whenever you can—don't allow guilt and worry about moral standards to interfere with your happiness. (And just ignore the fact that your "happiness" often brings misery.)

The so-called "mystery religions" in Greek and Roman culture affirmed that happiness could be found only in the gods, who alone were truly happy. Today's New Age beliefs have some similarities to these religions. New Age followers correctly see that happiness is found in a higher spiritual being or force, but they don't acknowledge the true God of the Bible.

When Christianity emerged, the appeal of Jesus' teachings was widespread. He emphasized truth and virtue, as did Stoicism, and the goodness of pleasures and happiness—including eating and drinking—as did Epicureanism. He also offered a true relationship with God, which the mystery religions fruitlessly sought. Just as he does today, Jesus offered the genuine happiness everyone wanted but had not found.

As a young believer, I often heard testimonies in which people happily recalled the day the gospel took hold of their hearts. Years later, it dawned on me that instead of only being happy about what Jesus did in the past (on the cross and at my conversion) and what he'll one day do (at his return), I should be happy in what he's doing today. The present is the only place we live. Happiness in God's Good News should be more than memories and anticipation. We should lay hold of it today and experience it here and now.

The psalmist was onto something when he said, "This is the day that the LORD has made; let us rejoice and be glad in it" (Psalm 118:24). Yes, in that context he spoke of one particular day, but God has ordained all the days of all his people (see Psalm 139:16). How much happier we'll be if we rejoice in what God is doing every day and every hour of our lives. Why wait many years—or until we're with the Lord—to look back and say, "God, I finally see that you were at work even in those hard times; I wish I would have trusted you then"?

I have a close friend who genuinely believes that nearly every meal, get-together, retreat, or vacation is the best he's ever experienced. This makes him fun to be with. His capacity to enjoy the moment and savor present happiness morphs into treasured memories of past happiness and anticipation of happiness to come. When he raves about today's delights, I smile and enter into his happiness. And this reminds me of God's own happiness and why I should enjoy Jesus not just in the biggest events of life, but also the smallest ones.

The true gospel cannot be improved upon. Theologian J. Gresham Machen (1881–1937) said, "In the gospel there is included all that the heart of man can wish."[4] What do we wish for most? Happiness.

Our happiness is certainly not the only thing the gospel is about. However, it's one of the wonderful things Christ accomplished through his redemptive work.

Circumstances constantly change, and good news comes

and goes, but we should look to God for happiness now. Why? Because the Good News of happiness has come, it is still here, and it will never go away!

Jesus, how can I ever thank you enough for the sacrifice you made in order to secure our salvation and open the pathway to endless happiness? I can't, and I know that, but I thank you sincerely for granting me an eternity to try.

-DAY 23-

Is seeking happiness unspiritual?

Everything God created is good, and nothing is to be rejected if it is received with thanksgiving, because it is consecrated by the word of God and prayer. 1 TIMOTHY 4:4-5, NIV

The faint, far-off results of those energies which God's creative rapture implanted in matter when He made the worlds are what we now call physical pleasures. . . . What would it be to taste at the fountainhead that stream of which even these lower reaches prove so intoxicating? Yet that, I believe, is what lies before us. The whole man is to drink joy from the fountain of joy. C. S. LEWIS

WHEN MY BOOK *HEAVEN* was published in 2004, one of my favorite professors from Bible college had serious objections. In the book I develop the doctrines of the Resurrection and the New Earth, and I envision what I believe Scripture teaches: an embodied life of loving and serving God as we reign over the New Earth.

I point out in the book the clear statements of Jesus that we will eat and drink on the New Earth. Depictions in Scripture lead logically to the conclusion that most of what we do in our current bodies on Earth we will do with greater happiness in our new bodies on the New Earth. I speculate, for instance, that as resurrected people on a resurrected Earth, we might invent, write, read, play games, and ride bikes.

This troubled my professor. Over coffee together, this godly man furrowed his brow and said, "When we can see God, why would we ever want to ride a bike?"

Both his countenance and his tone of voice told me that in his mind, seeing God was spiritual, while riding a bike was secular—almost sinful.

Respectfully, I asked him what Scripture means when it gives us this command: "Whether you eat or drink, or whatever you do, do all to the glory of God" (1 Corinthians 10:31). Eating and drinking are not only necessities but also physical pleasures that we're to do for God's glory. I told him that I ride my bike to God's glory in this life. And I worship God while joyfully playing tennis and snorkeling, just as I worship him while enjoying music, reading God's Word, and playing with dogs.

Why would we not be able to do that on the resurrected Earth? Couldn't a bike ride in the wondrous beauty of a new creation, alongside other worshipers of the King, lift our hearts to great praise, drawing us closer to him?

My beloved professor and I are just two voices in a larger

conversation about the role of the physical versus the spiritual when it comes to faith. For centuries, believers have wrestled with questions about how tangible, concrete, and physical our eternal happiness will be. When we see God, will we spend all our moments motionless, simply gazing at him? Or will we go about our days as physical beings, worshiping God while also enjoying each other's company and exploring the wonders of his creation?

Some Christians are wary of physical pleasure because of an unbiblical belief that the spirit realm is good while the material world is bad. I call this *Christoplatonism*, a term I coined in my book *Heaven*.[1] It's a widespread belief, sometimes spoken and sometimes not, that has plagued countless Christians and churches over the years, convincing people that physical pleasures are unspiritual and therefore that many of the things that make people happy are unworthy and suspect. The anti-body, anti-Earth, anti-culture assumptions of Christoplatonism naturally lend themselves to an anti-happiness viewpoint. Instead of spiritual being seen as the opposite of ungodly, it's seen as the opposite of physical and pleasurable.

Scripture contradicts this antagonism between body and spirit. God created body and spirit; both were marred by sin, and both are redeemed by Christ. Our bodies aren't prisons. Nor are they something we can occupy or abandon at will as a hermit crab does a shell. They're an essential and

God-designed aspect of our being. Our bodies weren't created to distract from our Creator but to disclose him. God made the material world not to hinder our walk with him but to facilitate it.

Why did God give us our ability to find joy in a cool swim and a hot shower, in listening to music and audiobooks, in eating pistachios, planting flowers, or running through a park? Why did he give us physical senses if not to know him better and to be far happier in him than we ever could be if he had instead made us disembodied spirits who couldn't enjoy physical pleasures?

God could have given us tasteless nutrients instead of filling the world with great-tasting food and giving us the taste buds to enjoy it. He could have easily devised some mechanistic means of conceiving children; instead, he devised the elaborate and pleasurable process of sexual relations. He could have looked at his creation and said, "It is functional." Instead he said, "It is very good!"

If we buy into, even subconsciously, the misguided perspective that bodies, the Earth, material things, and anything "secular" are automatically unspiritual, we will inevitably reject or spiritualize any biblical revelation about bodily resurrection or finding joy in God's physical creation.

We must be careful not to make idols out of God's provisions. But God is happy when we, with the proper perspective, enjoy his gifts to us. He's not up in Heaven frowning at us, saying, "Stop it—you should find joy only in me." This would be as foreign to our heavenly Father's nature as it would be to mine as an earthly father if I gave my daughters or grandchildren Christmas gifts, then pouted because they enjoyed them too much.

Yes, God wants us to find our joy in him. But a large part of that is through finding joy in what he has graciously provided for us, then consciously praising him for it.

Father God, thank you for our bodies, our senses, our emotions, and every other marvelous gift you've created. Give us wisdom to use these gifts for your glory and to fully appreciate and celebrate them—every day.

-DAY 24-

Is physical pleasure evil?

After my skin has been thus destroyed, yet in my flesh I shall see God. JOB 19:26

There is no good trying to be more spiritual than God. God never meant man to be a purely spiritual creature. That is why He uses material things like bread and wine to put the new life into us. We may think this rather crude and unspiritual. God does not: He invented eating. He likes matter. He invented it. C. S. LEWIS

MUCH OF WHAT I'VE READ about joy attempts to raise it to such a peak of spirituality that it disappears from the realm of mortals. But is it really possible for joy to be unemotional or separated from happiness? How can joy without happiness truly be joy? If joy isn't experienced as an emotion, how could it be experienced? Is the physical world so bad that we must spiritualize joy?

C. S. Lewis wrote,

Is physical pleasure evil?

*I know some muddle-headed Christians have talked
as if Christianity thought that sex, or the body, or
pleasure, were bad in themselves. But they were wrong.
Christianity is almost the only one of the great religions
which thoroughly approves of the body—which believes
that matter is good, that God Himself once took on a
human body, that some kind of body is going to be given
to us even in Heaven and is going to be an essential part
of our happiness, our beauty and our energy.*[1]

It's no coincidence that the apostle Paul's detailed defense of the physical resurrection was written to the church at Corinth. Corinthian believers were immersed in the Greek philosophies of Platonism and dualism, which perceived a dichotomy between the spiritual and physical realms.

Platonists see a disembodied soul as the ideal. The Bible, meanwhile, sees this division as unnatural and undesirable. We are unified beings. That's what makes bodily resurrection so vital. That's also why Paul said that if there is no Resurrection, "we are of all people most to be pitied" (1 Corinthians 15:19). The truth is, God intends for our bodies, once raised, to last as long as our souls.

Any views of the afterlife that settle for less than a full bodily resurrection—including Christoplatonism, reincarnation, and transmigration of the soul—are explicitly anti-Christian. The early church waged doctrinal wars against heresies that contradict the biblical account where God voices his pleasure with the entire physical realm, all of which he created and called "very good" (Genesis 1:31). Christ's resurrection itself repudiates the heresy of Christoplatonism (the idea that physical pleasures are unspiritual).

Sadly, Christoplatonism tears down that bridge to unbelievers by negating the value and goodness of not only the natural world but also the creativity of God's image bearers—their ability to build parks, playgrounds, zoos, dams, reservoirs, roads, monuments, greenhouses, and sculptures. People are sinners, to be sure, but is all human achievement nothing but sin? Does God hate creativity, art, architecture, business, music, and sports? Such thinking leaves believers with a shriveled view of both the present and the future. And it gives unbelievers a shriveled view of the gospel.

Some Christians' anti-physical worldview causes them to envision spirits stripped of bodies whose heavenly lives consist only of worship and service in a "higher plane" of disembodied angelic spirituality.

The movie *Babette's Feast* depicts a conservative Christian sect that scrupulously avoids "worldly" distractions.[2] They live out the unhappy philosophy of Christoplatonism—quick to judge, slow to rejoice, and convinced that celebration, pleasure, and laughter must be sinful.

Then Babette, once a gourmet cook in France, is forced by war to become a maid for the two women who lead this small group of austere believers. Babette unexpectedly inherits a significant sum of money, and out of gratitude for their kindness to her, she spends it all to prepare a fabulous dinner party for the elderly sisters and their friends.

Babette's Feast is a picture of God's extravagant grace. Touched by Babette's generosity and the great feast she prepared, the community's false guilt dissipates, and they begin to laugh, take delight, and truly enjoy the richness of God's provision. The movie illustrates the beauty of enjoying God's lavish, creative gifts with heartfelt gratitude. Over the many courses of this meal, these legalists gradually come to understand that when God and his gifts are the objects of our happiness, feasting and laughter and beauty draw us not away from God but to him.

How sad when the world doesn't see God as the source of the goodness of his creation. And how much sadder still when God's people don't see it either.

Oh, Father, you have promised us eternal life as *healthy, embodied people who have said a final good-bye to sin and suffering and who will be more capable of worship, friendship, love, discovery, work, and play than we've ever been—and therefore we'll be far happier than we've ever been! What joy to anticipate! Now open our eyes to the many good and wonderful physical gifts you give us on this side of eternity, and help us, with grateful hearts, to be happy with them and, in doing so, be happy with you.*

Can the search for happiness become an idol?

No one can serve two masters, for either he will hate the one and love the other, or he will be devoted to the one and despise the other. . . . But seek first the kingdom of God and his righteousness, and all these things will be added to you.
JESUS (MATTHEW 6:24, 33)

"Accepting Jesus" is not just adding Jesus. It is also subtracting the idols. RAY ORTLUND

DESPITE SHOWS SUCH AS *American Idol* and celebrities who earn the nickname "teen idols," most twenty-first-century Americans don't believe we're a nation of idol worshipers. The word *idol* conjures up images of primitive people offering sacrifices to crude carved images. Surely we're above that. Or are we?

In *Counterfeit Gods*, Tim Keller writes,

*Our contemporary society is not fundamentally
different from these ancient ones. Each culture is
dominated by its own set of idols. . . . We may not
physically kneel before the statue of Aphrodite, but
many young women today are driven into depression
and eating disorders by an obsessive concern over
their body image. We may not actually burn incense
to Artemis, but when money and career are raised
to cosmic proportions, we perform a kind of child
sacrifice, neglecting family and community to
achieve a higher place in business and gain more
wealth and prestige.*[1]

Idolatry began in Eden and has yet to end. In the first chapters of Genesis, God had no competition for the affection of his creatures. Humanity found its meaning, purpose, and happiness in God. God was God; everything else wasn't. And everyone knew it.

The Fall tragically changed that.

An idol is anything we praise, celebrate, fixate on, and look to for help that's not the true God. Scripture speaks strongly about the sin of idolatry: "Woe to those who go down to Egypt for help, and rely on horses, who trust in chariots because they are many, and in horsemen because they are very strong, but who do not look to the Holy One of Israel, nor seek the LORD!" (Isaiah 31:1, NKJV).

What does this have to do with happiness? Everything. Satan forfeited his own happiness, and he bitterly hates us—the objects of God's love. Since he's committed to making us just as miserable, the devil tempts us toward what will dishonor God by telling persuasive lies to convince us that the things that make us miserable will actually make us happy. After thousands of years of doing this, he's remarkably good at it. Jesus said of Satan, "When he lies, he speaks his native language, for he is a liar and the father of lies" (John 8:44, NIV).

Those who argue over whether to use cheese or peanut butter in a mousetrap agree on one thing: the stronger the attraction, the better the chance of catching what you're after. Every temptation uses false happiness as bait. A woman told me, "I left my family to find happiness. It didn't last, but I sacrificed for it the greatest happiness I'd ever known." In the name of momentary happiness, she made choices that brought her despair.

This is how the devil always works. Like anyone baiting a trap, he offers false happiness to bring utter ruin. How else could he get us to bite?

Everything that threatens to occupy the throne that only God can fill is an idol, and God calls us to ruthlessly dethrone these false gods: "This is what you are to do to them: Break down their altars, smash their sacred stones, cut down their Asherah poles and burn their idols in the fire" (Deuteronomy 7:5, NIV).

The happy life is to worship God as God—and not put anything or anyone else in his place. But in this fallen world, we can't simply affirm God as the source of happiness without dealing with the competition. Potential idols—loving relationships, success, hobbies, comfort, and wealth, to name a few—can be legitimate sources of happiness when enjoyed in their rightful position below God, but they become toxic when we elevate them above him. Hence, the search for happiness becomes an idol when, and only when, we try to find happiness apart from God.

John Piper says, "We all make a god out of what we take the most pleasure in."[2] The one way to avoid idolatry is to take the most pleasure in the one true God. As Christ-followers, we shouldn't be more tolerant of our idols than God was of Israel's. Once we recognize those idols, we can destroy them, exalting God alone. Only then can we know true and lasting happiness, for all lesser pleasures are only shadows.

Lord, you alone are God. We are not, nor is anything you've created. Help us to turn away from whatever threatens to take your place in our lives. We want happiness because of, never at the expense of, our relationship with you. Remind us that no happiness outside of you can possibly last. Reign supreme in our hearts, King Jesus!

-DAY 26-

How does seeing God accurately promote lasting happiness?

Oh, the joys of those who trust the LORD, who have no confidence in the proud or in those who worship idols.
PSALM 40:4, NLT

[We] must fight fire with fire. The fire of lust's pleasures must be fought with the fire of God's pleasures. . . . We must fight it with a massive promise of superior happiness. We must swallow up the little flicker of lust's pleasure in the conflagration of holy satisfaction. JOHN PIPER

YOUSSUF ISHMAELO (1857-1898), the "Terrible Turk," was an international wrestling phenomenon in the 1890s, known for demolishing his opponents. A suspicious man, he demanded his winnings in gold and strapped them into his belt, which he never removed. Then, while he was heading home from a victory in America, his ship sank.

Survivors remember Ishmaelo acting "like a wild beast."

With a dagger in hand, he forced his way through the frightened crowds who were waiting to board the lifeboats. He came to a fully loaded boat that was already being lowered. Ignoring the shouts of the crew, he jumped into it. His significant weight, together with the force of his leap, overturned the boat, and all its occupants were thrown into the sea. Ishmaelo, though a good swimmer, was dragged down under the weight of his $10,000 gold belt.[1]

Contrast Youssuf with Stanley Tam, who used wealth not as an idol but as a tool to worship God.

As a young door-to-door salesman, Tam met a farmer's wife who told him about Jesus. He soon placed his faith in Christ. With twenty-five dollars in his pocket, plus twelve dollars added by his father, he launched the United States Plastic Corp. Tam later sensed that God wanted to run the business with Tam as his employee. So he legally made God the majority owner of the business, gifting 51 percent of the company's stock to a nonprofit.

As the business prospered, Tam used all his profits to spread the gospel. His salary was a small fraction of what CEOs typically earn. He was careful not to rob God's glory and continually sought to give more to missions, ultimately contributing more than $140 million.

Tam was inspired to give through Jesus' story of the merchant who sold everything to purchase a pearl of great value (see Matthew 13:45-46). Like the man in Christ's story, Tam joyfully placed 100 percent ownership of United States Plastic Corp. into a foundation that established churches in developing countries.

He guarded himself against idolatry by giving God prominence in his life. As I write this, Stanley Tam is a hundred-year-old man who has lived a happy life and is anticipating the words, "Well done, my good and faithful servant."[2]

We choose where to place our affections—either on God or on God substitutes. Joshua called on the Israelites to follow God intentionally: "Choose for yourselves this day whom you will serve, whether the gods which your fathers served that were on the other side of the River, or the gods of the Amorites, in whose land you dwell. But as for me and my house, we will serve the LORD" (Joshua 24:15, NKJV). People will not turn from idols to the true God unless they know how great and satisfying God is and what destruction and misery idols bring.

Tim Keller states, "Sin isn't only doing bad things, it is more fundamentally making good things into ultimate things. Sin is building your life and meaning on anything, even a very good thing, more than on God. Whatever we build our life on will drive us and enslave us. Sin is primarily idolatry."[3]

We worship whatever we believe will ultimately make us happy. But it's possible to worship the God of the Bible while believing things about him that aren't true. So we worship a false object in a way that makes even what we call "God" into an idol.

It's common to hear people say, "I like to think of God not as my judge but as my papa," or "I like to think of Jesus as my friend, not my master." But he's all the things Scripture reveals him to be, all the time, including Judge, Father, Friend, and Master. His attributes aren't a smorgasbord for finicky Christians to choose what they want and leave the rest untouched.

If we take one attribute of God—his love, for instance—and divorce it from his other attributes, including his holiness, we end up worshiping our own distorted concept of love instead of the true God. He is indeed love, but love as he defines it, not as we do. And he has many other qualities as well. We're to worship the God of love and holiness, grace and truth, justice and compassion, wrath and happiness.

Jesus is not only the Lamb of God or the Good Shepherd. He's those and much more. The gentle, compassionate Jesus is also the Jesus who drove the merchant-thieves from the Temple and spoke condemnation against self-righteous religious leaders. Were Jesus as meek and mild as many think, he never would have been crucified. But his less popular qualities so outraged people that they nailed him to a cross.

We should believe all that Scripture says about God—the parts that make sense to our finite, little minds and those that don't. Only then can we avoid idolatrous thoughts about him.

A life characterized by an eternal perspective focuses on long-term happiness. In saying no to idolatrous pleasures and false perceptions of God and in saying yes to the pleasures of God—present and future—we choose what is for both his glory and our good.

———————————

Lord, help us to love and serve you with all that we are. Keep our hearts free from idols and false ideas about you. Help us not to settle for counterfeit substitutes but yearn for more and more of you. We need—and want—to exalt you as our one and only God.

Who or what is our primary source of happiness?

To the LORD your God belong the heavens, even the highest heavens, the earth and everything in it.
DEUTERONOMY 10:14, NIV

As there is the most heat nearest to the sun, so there is the most happiness nearest to Christ. CHARLES SPURGEON

HAPPINESS CAN'T BE bigger than its source. God is primary; all other forms of happiness—relationships, created things, and material pleasures—are secondary. If we don't consciously see God as their source, these secondary things intended for enjoyment can master us.

Things such as winning a game, a promotion, or a contest; or taking a new job or a vacation are too small to bring big happiness. God, on the other hand, "satisfies the longing soul, and the hungry soul he fills with good things" (Psalm 107:9). We're finite and fallen, and we lack what's required for happiness. All those who look within themselves for pleasures and delight are doomed to misery. We just aren't big enough and good enough to supply the happiness we crave!

Christ-followers enjoy what God provides first and foremost because they enjoy the God who provides them. Unlike us, God is infinite and without flaws. Secondary things bring some joy, but God alone is our "exceeding joy" (Psalm 43:4). Scottish theologian Samuel Rutherford (1600–1661) wrote, "It is the infinite Godhead that must allay the sharpness of your hunger after happiness, otherwise there shall still be a want of satisfaction to your desires."[1]

Secondary things are not incidental or unimportant—they're God's gifts to draw us to him—so we should never disdain the created world. But by putting God first and his creation second, the world and its beauties become instruments of joy and worship. We love them better when we love God more than them.

Why do we watch the World Series or the Olympics? Why do we go to the Grand Canyon, the Alps, or the ocean? Why do we want to get near bigness and beauty and magnificence? Because we find happiness in beholding what's greater than ourselves. It's what we're made for: an infinitely great, happy-making God.

When an atheist enjoys the cool breeze of a sunny autumn day as he writes his treatise on God's nonexistence, the source of his pleasure is God. For God is the author of the universe itself: the Earth, cool breezes, sunny days, the atheist made in God's image, the physical sensations that give the capacity to enjoy nature, and even the powers of rational thought the atheist uses to argue against God.

One of the keys to enjoying life is connecting the dots between our happiness and God as its provider, as well as between our happiness and God's own happiness. When I run with my dog or look at Jupiter dominating the sky over Mount Hood, I experience happiness. Unbelievers are capable of enjoying happiness in exactly the same things, but their happiness can't be as immense or enduring, because they stop short of recognizing the one whose overflowing reservoir of happiness has spilled over into his creation.

This helps us understand what Asaph says in Psalm 73: "Whom have I in heaven but you? And there is nothing on earth that I desire besides you" (verse 25). Is Asaph saying he doesn't desire food, water, clothes, shelter, friendship, and laughter? No. He's saying, in essence, "Of the many things I desire, at the core of all of them is God himself. Therefore, all that I desire is summed up in God alone."

As I write this, I'm looking up from my computer at a photo I took underwater. It reminds me of the sheer delight of my unforgettable ninety-minute encounter with a wonderful monk seal I named Molly.

Whenever I look at Molly's photo, my heart fills with joyful memories and longing for the New Earth's joy and the days that await us. That anticipation gives me a harvest of happiness today. Of course, many people who don't know God love to snorkel and dive. They're truly moved by the enchanting beauty of the reef.

But an immense part of my happiness as I snorkel is knowing God, the primary, who made all these secondary wonders. I sense his presence with me—both when I'm out in his ocean and as I sit in my home remembering his nearness, both then and now. This is a shared experience between my God and me, and even as I type, the memories of countless hours spent in the water together with him, enjoying his beautiful underwater kingdom, bring joyful tears to my eyes. The beautiful coral reef and its wondrous creatures don't draw me away from God—they draw me to him. But if I were to worship them and not the God who made them, I would not only displease him, I would diminish and ruin them.

In the movie *The Avengers*, Thor's brother, the evil Loki, weary of the Incredible Hulk, says to him in a commanding voice, "Enough! . . . I am a god, you dull creature!" The Hulk, unimpressed, picks up Loki with one hand and gives him a merciless thrashing, pounding him into the ground. As he walks away, the Hulk turns back toward Loki, looking disgusted, and mutters, "Puny god." Loki, utterly defeated, gives a pathetic little squeak.

All idols are not only false gods but also puny gods. The very gifts of God that can bring us great joy become dismally small when we make them primary. Only the true God is big enough to bear the weight of all our happiness, and the larger we see him, the bigger our happiness in him.

In the mid-1600s, Puritan John Gibbon said, "God alone is enough, but without him, nothing [is enough] for thy happiness."[2] Whether or not we're conscious of it, since God is the fountainhead of happiness, the search for happiness is always the search for God.

Father, we can't even begin to fathom how enormous your capacity for happiness is. But we're grateful you want to share that happiness with us. Expand our reservoir and fill us so full that we overflow and share your joy with those in this hurting world who need it most.

-DAY 28-

How can pleasure point us to God?

Taste and see how good the LORD is! The one who takes refuge in him is truly happy! PSALM 34:8, CEB

God cannot give us a happiness and peace apart from Himself, because it is not there. There is no such thing. C. S. LEWIS

THE MORE WE ENJOY pure pleasure, the closer we are to seeing God. If this seems wrong to us, we're not understanding who God is and how he created us in the world.

In *The Screwtape Letters*, the demon Wormwood reports to Screwtape that he has lost his subject to God ("the Enemy"). Screwtape asks, "Could you not have seduced him?" He points out Wormwood's error:

> *You . . . allowed the patient to read a book he really enjoyed, because he enjoyed it and not in order to make clever remarks about it to his new friends. In the second place, you allowed him to walk down to the old mill and have tea there—a walk through country he*

really likes. . . . In other words you allowed him two real
positive Pleasures. Were you so ignorant as not to see
the danger of this?[1]

Genuine pleasures, even simple ones, can point people to
God. Satan's strategy is to divorce pleasure from its logical connection with God. In doing so, he robs God of glory and us of
happiness! If he can divorce God from pleasure, delight, and happiness, he can poison our view of God and make the Christian life
appear unattractive and sin more attractive. If we believe there's
happiness without God, then we'll seek happiness without God.

I've heard it said, "We should set our minds on God—no
one and nothing else." It sounds spiritual, but is it accurate?
Clearly not, since Scripture commands us to think about
"whatever is true, whatever is honorable, whatever is just,
whatever is pure, whatever is lovely, whatever is commendable, if there is any excellence, if there is anything worthy
of praise, think about these things" (Philippians 4:8). These
true, honorable, just, pure, lovely, commendable, excellent,
and praiseworthy things aren't God, but they're rooted in his
character. We should trace them back to him as we'd trace a
sunbeam back to the sun.

So by all means, we should contemplate and enjoy all created goodness. But when we do so, we should thankfully worship God as its source, so that in thinking of and delighting in
every good thing, we'll be thinking of and delighting in our Lord.

The world is full of desperate people thirsting for gladness and trying to derive it from what cannot satisfy us for long. They eagerly drink from contaminated water surrounded by huge signs with neon letters flashing "Fun!" Sometimes there's no fun at all, and often the fun quickly evaporates, leaving shame and regret. (If the signs were accurate, they would say "Deadly poison!")

What people long for and desperately need can be found only in the "fountain of living waters"—God himself. God laments over the poor choices we make: "My people have committed two evils: they have forsaken me, the fountain of living waters, and hewed out cisterns for themselves, broken cisterns that can hold no water" (Jeremiah 2:13).

When I'm thirsty, I don't look up water on Wikipedia. I don't go to social media to find out what others say about water. I don't drink out of the nearest puddle. I go to the faucet and satisfy my thirst by drinking some of the world's best water from the Bull Run water system where I live in Oregon.

I find God to be pure, refreshing, and satisfying. My happiest days are those I drink most deeply of him. I also know that if I don't drink of him, I will drink something else—something that will leave me thirsty, dissatisfied, and sick. For idols cannot satisfy. Evangelist George Whitefield (1714–1770) wrote, "I drank of God's pleasure as out of a river. Oh that all were made partakers of this living water."[2]

Jonestown was a socialist community in South America.

In 1978, after murdering a US congressman and four others, Jim Jones gathered his cult members, who had relocated from the United States to Guyana, and served them a grape-flavored drink laced with cyanide, thereby killing himself and 912 of his followers.

Hence the expression "Don't drink the Kool-Aid," which means, "Don't follow anyone blindly—if you do, it'll likely kill you." This is good advice for gullible people who are prone to believe that counterfeits will really deliver happiness.

Most offers of happiness are deceptions. People were wrong to trust Jim Jones. But we are right to trust Jesus, God's Son, who went to the cross to bring us into relationship with God. Jesus is fully worthy of our trust, and he makes this offer: "If anyone thirsts, let him come to me and drink. Whoever believes in me, as the Scripture has said, 'Out of his heart will flow rivers of living water'" (John 7:37-38).

We're free to be unhappy. We're free to search for happiness where it can't be found. What we're not free to do is reinvent God, the universe, or ourselves so that what isn't from God will bring us happiness.

Are you thirsty for happiness—for meaning, peace, contentment? Jesus invites you to join hundreds of millions throughout history and across the globe, and a multitude of those now living in the visible presence of the fountain of living waters, to come to him and drink the best water in the universe—the only refreshment that will ever fully and eternally satisfy.

Jesus, you offer us living water. Draw us to taste of you daily and see that you are good so that we will come back to you to be satisfied again and again. Increase our thirst for you, and increase our satisfaction in being with you so that we will drink deeper of you each day. May we experience your refreshment so that we never settle for those broken cisterns that can hold no water.

How can enjoying happiness in God's creation draw us to God?

*Every good gift and every perfect gift is from above, coming
down from the Father of lights with whom there is no variation
or shadow due to change.*   JAMES 1:17

*God is the only source of happiness and joy, and no creature
is or can be a source of happiness independently of Him. But
He can and does make use of creatures to adorn, perfect, and
complete the happiness of the whole man.*

FLORENTIN J. BOUDREAUX

TWO SERIOUSLY ILL MEN occupied the same hospital room.
The man next to the window was able to sit up, while the other
couldn't.

Each day the man by the window described in picturesque
detail what he saw—including a lake, ducks, and children
sailing model boats. This meant the world to his roommate,

who had no outside view. Witnessing these sights secondhand brought him daily happiness.

Eventually the man by the window died. His saddened roommate requested a move to the bed by the window. He couldn't wait to enjoy all the sights his roommate had described. But as he eagerly looked outside for the first time all he saw was an old brick wall.

Perspective makes all the difference. His roommate had been able to see, in his mind's eye, life beyond the wall. Some prisoners, surrounded by bare walls, see in their imaginations the world's true beauty. But many "free people" are surrounded by rich beauty yet day after day, year after year, fail to see it. Who is happier?

J. R. R. Tolkien wrote in *The Fellowship of the Ring*: "The world is indeed full of peril, and in it there are many dark places; but still there is much that is fair, and though in all lands love is now mingled with grief, it grows perhaps the greater."[1]

The better I know Jesus, the more I see him all around me—in people, animals, places, and objects. But if I hadn't studied his Word and reflected on his character over the years, I wouldn't have known what to look for. A student of insects or birds can see dozens of fascinating specimens on a short walk. Another person on the same walk, not having learned to observe, can miss them altogether.

Scripture paints a picture of how we should think about

God in our daily lives: we should be talking about (and to) God throughout the day, teaching ourselves and our children to see him in everything (see Deuteronomy 6:1-7).

Two of my grandsons love football and speak tirelessly of professional players. So Nanci and I enter into their world. We name those we consider the best players and say, "Isn't it amazing that God has given each person special gifts to use for his glory, and the rest of us get to enjoy it?" In this way, we see God's master craftsmanship in the beauty of life. When we see an athlete who honors Christ, we encourage our grandsons with his or her example. When we see ugliness in an athlete who glorifies himself, we see the Curse at work, and it's another teaching opportunity.

Consider the brightest "stars" in the sky—which are actually the planets Venus, Jupiter, Mars, and Saturn. Unlike the true stars we see, which are far away and therefore dimmer, these planets don't shine with their own light; they are bright only because they reflect the sun.

Likewise, the moon is a beautiful sight, but it doesn't generate light on its own. It merely reflects it. *Merely* makes the reflection sound trivial, but this is actually a magnificent phenomenon. The moon was made to glorify the sun, and when it does, it shares in the sun's glory. (If the moon were able to talk, wouldn't we think it foolish if we heard it congratulate itself for how brightly it shines?)

So it is with all secondary sources of happiness. Things

such as art, music, literature, sports, careers, and hobbies generate no light on their own. The light they bring comes from "the Father of lights" (James 1:17).

I don't value the planets and moon less because they don't shine by their own light. Likewise, I don't devalue my wife, my children, my grandchildren, my coworkers, or my dog because they're secondary to God and reflect him. On the contrary, I value them all the more because the God who is primary has made them who and what they are, and he has endowed them with worth that makes them far more important than if they were merely random accidents with a flickering light of their own.

Happiness can be sought in thousands of places, but it can be found in only one. That source is God, who incredibly is "Christ in you" (Colossians 1:27). He is big enough to create the galaxies, yet he dwells in each of us who know him.

God, expand our ability to see your reflection in every good thing. And help us to love that reflection because the face we see is yours. What happiness awaits us as we more clearly see you in and through all the good and perfect gifts you give!

When are good things wrong, and when are they right?

As for the rich in this present age, charge them not to be haughty, nor to set their hopes on the uncertainty of riches, but on God, who richly provides us with everything to enjoy.

1 TIMOTHY 6:17

What should be rejoiced in, if not the Lord of life himself, who is the everlasting joy and glory of the saints?

RICHARD BAXTER

WHEN WE WORSHIP God as God, everything else falls into place—good food and drink are delightful; friendship is fulfilling; marital sex can be deeply satisfying; and work, hobbies, sports, music, and entertainment can all enrich our lives as intended.

If I'm not happy in God when I see a waterfall or hear a great symphony or see a child playing in a mud puddle or watch a dog chasing his tail, then I'll not be happy in God when I attend church, read the Bible, or pray. I may congratulate myself for my spirituality when my eyes are on myself rather than him, but that's being pleased with my supposed piety, not being happy in God.

Idolatry is looking to the secondary as the source of happiness rather than as a conduit. What's good ceases to be good when we give it the prominence that should be reserved for God.

The child who loves to play basketball as one part of his life can one day look back with fond memories and look forward to what's next. The adult who makes basketball the center of his life still ruminates on his childhood successes and failures, and is devastated when his kids don't make the team or when his favorite team loses. The problem isn't basketball; the problem is turning basketball (or anything else) into the main thing. If it's the main thing, it's our god.

Is it really okay for me to enjoy my family, taco salad, books, and biking? Yes, if they're part of enjoying God and not alternatives to him. As long as they remain under him and I thank him for the happiness he brings through them, they can't compete with him.

While taking a break from writing about happiness, I experienced a series of events that illustrated the relationship between the secondary and primary.

First, I stood on our deck and looked up at the cold night sky, filled with the familiar stars I've known and loved since childhood. Then I returned to the warm house and pondered the immensity and beauty of the universe.

Once inside, I looked at a chair with Nanci's Bible beside it. She's part of a team that writes and edits lessons for our church's weekly women's Bible study, and that day she'd led the study. I thanked God for her, my best friend and a woman of the Word. I pondered how Nanci and I have known each other for forty-seven years and that I love her more than ever. I marveled at God's grace in bringing us together and thanked him for our two wonderful daughters and our grandchildren. At that moment Maggie, our golden retriever, sidled up and put her paw on my knee.

I stroked Maggie's head, and she gazed into my eyes and sighed deeply. I thanked God for dogs and for Maggie in particular, and I contemplated how God reveals glimpses of himself through his creation. Maggie is loyal to me; God is loyal. She's beautiful; God is the maker of all beauty. Maggie makes me happy many times a day. But because I understand Maggie's true nature and role, I realize it is God, in his kindness, who makes me happy through her. So I poured out my heart in gratitude to him.

All these secondary things are important because they point me to God, the primary. During that break from writing about happiness, I realized I am profoundly happy—and that all this happiness comes from the hand of God!

I love snorkeling and taking underwater photos of God's

sea creatures. I look at photos years later, some of them hanging in our home and my office, and they take me back to those magical moments of discovery. Through the photos, raccoon butterfly fish and Christmas wrasses reach out to me from their homes in the reef. The pictures rekindle my original delight when, peering into the dark shadows, I saw a puffer fish peeking back with huge eyes and a frogfish masterfully disguising itself as part of the reef. I remember the sudden discovery of a moray eel lurking behind two giant sea turtles and the thrill of seeing one whitetip reef shark, then five, emerging from a cave below me. I recall swimming in the open ocean and suddenly becoming part of a pod of dolphins as they wove their way next to and around me, seemingly adopting me as part of their pod. What wonder and worship!

The simple, daily cultivation of God-consciousness has had a central role in the increasing happiness I've experienced over the years. I often have coffee with God, and sometimes I have a meal alone with him. Occasionally when I'm praying, and those who've read my novel *Safely Home* may relate to this, I pull out a chair for Jesus and envision him occupying it (not only did he sit in chairs, he also built them!). I talk to him. I'm not pretending Jesus is with me at lunch or when I pray; I simply believe his promise that he really is with me and I act in keeping with it. If you want to be happy, put meaning to the sometimes empty phrase "spending time with God."

When we invite God into our happiness, we become aware

of how he invites us into his. The happiest times of my life are when I've entered into the happiness of God—not only through Bible study, prayer, and church, but also when reading a good book, laughing with a friend, running, biking, and enjoying the wonders of his creation. It's a glorious thing to know God and love him through loving the world he has made—and anticipating the day when that world will be all he intends it to be.

God, thank you for your incredible creativity in making the beautiful, sprawling, detailed, and fascinating universe you've placed us in. The small portion we've discovered is enough to surprise and delight us for ages to come. How we long for the day when the adventures begin anew and without hindrance—an eternity of discovering still more about you through the wonders of the New Heaven and New Earth!

-DAY 31-

How does creation demonstrate God's happiness?

I am so happy I found my lost sheep. Let us celebrate!
LUKE 15:6, GNT

"And God saw everything that he had made, and behold, it was very good." I take this to mean that God was delighted with his work. When he looked at it, it gave him pleasure. He was pleased and happy with his creative effort. JOHN PIPER

I'VE NEVER BEEN to Iguazú Falls, on the border of Brazil and Argentina. But I've watched astounding videos that offer a glimpse of its wonders.

The falls are 1.7 miles across, with many small islands dividing the torrent of water into separate cataracts and waterfalls. Depending on the water level, there are between 150 and 300 of these falls, varying from about 200 to 270 feet high. I've witnessed the power of Niagara Falls firsthand, but the volume of the cascading waters of Iguazú Falls can be up to twenty times greater. (Upon visiting Iguazú Falls, Eleanor Roosevelt reportedly exclaimed, "Poor Niagara!"[1])

For those who believe in God, wonders like these are compelling evidence of the one who takes delight in his creation.

If we are going to fully trust God, it's vital that we believe in a happy God who cares deeply for our welfare and is active in creation and redemption.

A. W. Tozer depicted the happiness of God as seen in his creation:

> *God is not only pleased with Himself, delighted with His own perfection and happy in His work of creating and redeeming, but He is also enthusiastic. There is an enthusiasm in the Godhead, and there is enthusiasm in creation. . . . This infinite God is enjoying Himself. Somebody is having a good time in heaven and earth and sea and sky. Somebody is painting the sky. Somebody is making trees to grow . . . causing the ice to melt . . . and the fish to swim and the birds to sing. . . . Somebody's running the universe.*[2]

Is God happy about the animals he has made? Take a look at this: "Do you give the horse his might? Do you clothe his neck with a mane? . . . He paws in the valley and exults in his strength. . . . He laughs at fear and is not dismayed. . . . With fierceness and rage he swallows the ground; he cannot stand still at the sound of the trumpet. When the trumpet sounds, he says 'Aha!'" (Job 39:19, 21-22, 24-25).

Isn't God's utter delight in horses obvious? Since he finds pleasure and happiness in animals, we shouldn't feel "unspiritual" when we do. To animal-loving unbelievers, we can say, "I believe in a God who not only made those animals but also delights in them!"

Does God have a sense of humor? He created the giraffe, the camel, the hippopotamus, and the duck-billed platypus. If you need more proof, look online at photos of animals such as the proboscis monkey, the star-nosed mole, the pink fairy armadillo, the Dumbo octopus, the sucker-footed bat, the blobfish, or my personal favorite, the axolotl.[3] I've done this several times with my grandsons, enjoying shrieking laughter and great conversations about God's happiness and sense of humor.

Had we been able to watch God spin the galaxies into existence, fashion this planet, and make animals and the first humans (perhaps one day we'll go back and see all this), we'd surely have seen his happiness and the pleasures he intended for us.

Our view of God's happiness with and in his creation will inevitably determine our view of the gospel's depth and breadth. The implications are far reaching. If God is happy only with limited aspects of his creative work and hostile or indifferent to most of it, including the culture developed by his image bearers, then there's far less left to bring him glory. But suppose he still loves his fallen creation and desires not to destroy it but to redeem it so that he and we might forever take delight in it!

Charles Spurgeon said,

Let a man truly know the Grace of our Lord Jesus Christ, and he will be a happy man! And the deeper he drinks into the spirit of Christ, the more happy will he become! That religion which teaches misery to be a duty is false upon the very face of it, for God, when He made the world, studied the happiness of His creatures. You cannot help thinking, as you see everything around you, that God has diligently, with the most strict attention, sought ways of pleasing man. He has not just given us our absolute necessities, He has given us more—not simply the useful, but even the ornamental! The flowers . . . the stars . . . the hill and the valley—all these things were intended not merely because we needed them, but because God would show us how He loved us and how anxious He was that we should be happy!

Now, it is not likely that the God who made a happy world would send a miserable salvation! He who is a happy Creator will be a happy Redeemer![4]

———

Lord Jesus, you are the Word—you spun the galaxies into being and spoke life into your creation. What joy we feel when we see your handiwork and realize that you made it not just to keep it to yourself but to share it with us. I can imagine you laughing out loud as you formed some of this world's crazy-looking creatures. Some of them, in the deepest part of the oceans and perhaps in other worlds, haven't even been discovered yet. Thank you for the glorious variety of gifts you've so kindly entrusted to us. And thank you that in the ages to come you won't cease to be a Creator of what's new and wonderful!

-DAY 32-

What makes our Father happy?

How precious is your steadfast love, O God! The children of mankind . . . feast on the abundance of your house, and you give them drink from the river of your delights.   PSALM 36:7-8

God transcendent in heaven and immanent in all creation is supremely happy . . . always has been so, and forever will be.
ROBERT DUNCAN CULVER

GOD CREATED THE UNIVERSE out of nothing. But he doesn't create love, holiness, and happiness as separate entities. Rather, those ever-existing attributes emanate from his own nature.

Nine qualities are listed as the fruit of the Spirit, the first being love and the second joy (see Galatians 5:22-23). There is "joy in the Holy Spirit" (Romans 14:17). Jesus was "full of joy through the Holy Spirit" (Luke 10:21, NIV). Joy is not merely something God brings; joy is someone God is.

If we see God as happy, suddenly the command for us to

"find your joy in him at all times" (Philippians 4:4, PHILLIPS) makes sense. God is saying, in essence, "Be as I am." Paralleling "Be holy, because I am holy" (1 Peter 1:16, NIV), the answer to the question "Why should God's children be happy?" is "Because our Father is happy." And his children should naturally bear his likeness.

In first-century Palestine, entering into someone's home and happiness meant removing dirty sandals to bathe and put on clean clothes and then enjoy a delicious feast with a delightful host. Visualize an estate owner and host who somehow exists in three persons. Suppose his guests witness, with utter delight, these three persons enjoying each other with eternal and infinite happiness. Now imagine that the guests don't just observe this delightful relationship but are invited to join it.

What we've just supposed is what God has actually done. Along with countless other sons and daughters of the King, we'll celebrate God without end and be happy with him and in him.

Jonathan Edwards said, "The happiness of the Deity, as all other true happiness, consists in love and society."[1] In other words, the God who is three in one has always been engaged in happy relationships. He didn't first enter into a happy society through creating and loving us—he already had that society, but he graciously includes us in his happiness.

In Zephaniah 3:14, God calls upon his people to be glad

using four different Hebrew words that convey happiness: "Sing aloud [with joy, or *rinnah*[2]], O daughter of Zion; shout [for joy, or *ruah*[3]], O Israel! Rejoice [*samach*] and exult [*alaz*] with all your heart."

The gladness described here is over the top—surely a God who isn't happy would never call his people to such happiness. But three verses later, in Zephaniah 3:17, we see an even more remarkable statement, which also contains four happiness words. This time, however, all four terms are used not of God's people but of God himself: "The LORD your God is in your midst, a mighty one who will save; he will rejoice [*sus*] over you with gladness [*simchah*]; he will quiet you by his love; he will exult over you [*gyl*] with loud singing [*rinnah*]." There's more of the happiness, tenderness, and love of God for us in this single verse than we can wrap our minds around. In fact, this understanding about God's delight in us is the rock-solid foundation for the fourfold happiness he calls on his people to experience three verses earlier. We're accustomed to thinking of God as angry or saddened by us. But here we're told, four times over, of God's happiness over us! Tozer said of this passage, "God is happy if nobody else is."[4]

While Zephaniah was speaking to his fellow Israelites, it's no stretch to say that today's believers, the church, are also God's people. Certainly God's nature hasn't changed, so everything Zephaniah 3:17 says about God's happiness remains true. As he rejoiced over Israel, he also rejoices over us.

This verse alone, even if there weren't hundreds of others that affirm the same truth, should be sufficient to convince us that God is happy with us.

———————

Father, *thank you for being happy and creating us with the ability to enjoy that happiness with you. To think of you singing over us is mind boggling. Help us learn more about your happiness, and let it fill our minds and our hearts.*

-DAY 33-

Is calling God happy blasphemous ... or at least disrespectful?

You [God] make [David] happy with the joy of your presence.
PSALM 21:6, CEB

Joy is the most infallible sign of the presence of God.
PIERRE TEILHARD DE CHARDIN

ABRAHAM LINCOLN'S advisers recommended that he include a particular man in his presidential cabinet. When he refused, they asked why.

"I don't like the man's face," Lincoln replied.

Surprised, someone insisted, "But the poor man isn't responsible for his face." Lincoln responded, "Every man over forty is responsible for his face."[1]

Lincoln wasn't talking about a person's physical beauty; he was saying that the heart's condition always makes its way to the face. "A happy heart makes the face cheerful"

(Proverbs 15:13, NIV). If that's true of us, isn't it true of the God whose image we bear?

Typically we associate God's face with holiness. But doesn't it also reflect his love, compassion, and happiness?

God says of his people, "Their faces will shine with happiness about all the good things from the LORD" (Jeremiah 31:12, NCV). This suggests that God's face shines with a happiness so great it spills onto the faces of those who love him. (Certainly an unhappy God wouldn't make his people's faces shine with happiness.)

God told Moses what Aaron and the priests were to say to the people: "The LORD bless you and keep you; the LORD make his face shine on you and be gracious to you; the LORD turn his face toward you and give you peace" (Numbers 6:24-26, NIV). How do you envision a face that shines on you and is gracious to you and gives you peace? Would such a face be stern and hostile, or pleasant and happy?

Gaining an understanding of God's happiness is so vital and yet foreign to the thinking of many believers. Charles Spurgeon said of 1 Timothy 1:11, "The Gospel . . . is the Gospel of happiness. It is called, 'the glorious Gospel of the blessed God.' A more correct translation would be, 'the happy God.' Well, then, adorn the Gospel by being happy!"[2]

When writing to Timothy, Paul didn't simply talk about the gospel; he referred to the good news of the happy God. This good news comes from God and relates to his glory—he is not just any god but the happy God. God's happiness is included here as part of the gospel's good news. This corresponds to the gospel being prophesied as the "good news of happiness" (Isaiah 52:7), which the angel told the shepherds, in words that mean the same thing, was "good news of great joy" (Luke 2:10). The degree of happiness in the good news is dependent on the degree of happiness of the originator and sender of that good news—God himself.

Occam's razor is the philosophical rule that the simplest explanation is most likely true. It argues that the more assumptions required, the more unlikely the account. In 1 Timothy 1:11, the simplest explanation is that, under the inspiration of God's Spirit, Paul called God happy precisely because God is happy!

When I've shared from Scripture the truth of God's happiness, people who've long been Christians are sometimes initially skeptical, assuming this is a modern attempt to twist the Bible's meaning. But once they see the truth, they're both surprised and delighted.

Sadly, few churches teach that God is happy—or wants us to be happy. In fact, we're often taught the opposite. The result is silencing or contradicting the biblical revelation of one of God's great attributes, at immense loss to the church, families, and individuals.

I've heard people say that calling God happy makes them uncomfortable. Others maintain that using the word *blessed* instead of *happy* imparts more dignity to God. Should we refuse to call God what he, in his inspired Word, calls himself? Isn't that censoring God?

In Jesus' parable, when the prodigal's father runs across the field to greet his repentant son, commentators point out that it was undignified for men in the ancient Middle East to run.[3] But in his overflowing happiness, the father, who represents God, disregards his dignity to shower grace upon his repentant son.

God sees no incompatibility between his dignity and his happiness. Why should we?

As the only infinite being in the universe, God has within himself not only infinite holiness, love, and goodness but also infinite peace, joy, and delight. He truly is the happy God. God's unhappiness with sin is temporary, because sin itself is a temporary aberration—one dealt with by Christ. Happiness, however, is the underlying nature of the timeless God. His happiness, without beginning, eternally preceded sin's birth and will forever continue after sin's death.

My heartfelt belief that God is happy motivates me to love him more and know him better. I like being with happy people— who doesn't? I'm motivated to spend time with them and look forward to getting to know them better. The idea of spending extended time with someone who is unhappy sounds daunting and disheartening. Yet that's what "eternal life" means to many people: living forever with an unhappy God.

I'd much rather spend not only eternity but also my present

life accompanied by, indwelt by, and empowered by a happy God—one who understands my desire for happiness because he, too, experiences and thoroughly enjoys his happiness.

Of course, that I want something doesn't make it true. What proves it is true is that God reveals his happiness in his Word. Let's state it emphatically and believe it with all our hearts: God is happy!

———

Lord, help us to enjoy and contemplate and praise you for your happiness. And in doing so, help us experience what it means to delight in you daily. Happiness pervades you and radiates from you, and we're grateful that you wanted to share your happiness with us, who you created in your image. Thank you, our happy God, for going to unimaginable lengths to secure forever our own happiness by entering into your own happiness.

When did happiness begin?

This is my beloved Son, with whom I am well pleased.
MATTHEW 3:17

There is a concurrence of all the persons of the Holy Trinity in the happiness of heaven: the Father, Son and Holy Ghost are equally the fountain of that eternal blessedness the saints enjoy. WILLIAM BATES

"TEAM HOYT," a father-son duo, was inducted into the Ironman Hall of Fame. Dick Hoyt and his son Rick, who was born with cerebral palsy, started competing together in marathons and triathlons in 1977, when Rick was fifteen. They participated in more than 1,100 events spanning four decades. In triathlons, Dick swam, pulling Rick in a special boat; he bicycled with Rick attached to a custom-made seat; and he ran, pushing Rick in a wheelchair. They participated in seventy-two marathons and six Ironman triathlons together. They biked and ran across the United States, completing 3,735 miles in forty-five days.

When did happiness begin?

The Hoyts continued to compete until 2014, when Dick was in his midseventies and Rick was in his midfifties.[1] They inspired millions of people who watched them race. The bond this father and son experienced in a sport known for its individualism was a source of great joy for both of them, and for those who witnessed their beautiful relationship and achievements.

The most ancient team in the universe consists of three persons: Father, Son, and Holy Spirit.

In his book *Delighting in the Trinity*, Michael Reeves writes, "The Trinity is the governing center of all Christian belief, the truth that shapes and beautifies all others. The Trinity is the cockpit of all Christian thinking."[2] Yet strangely, the Trinity is rarely discussed in the many Christian books on joy I've read.

The only way God's happiness or love could be without beginning is if there exists within God himself a reason for and object of his happiness and love. Baptist pastor and theologian Augustus Strong (1836–1921) said, "Love is an impossible exercise to a solitary being."[3]

God is one, but he is not solitary. Since God is loving and happy within himself, he didn't create the world out of need. It's easy to imagine that a God full of love and happiness might wish to express those emotions in the form of a universe, angels, people, and animals. They could enjoy his happiness, and he could enjoy them. But God does not need his creation in order for his happiness to be complete.

The doctrine of the Trinity beautifully resolves the

apparent problem of God's love preexisting any object of his love. Likewise, his happiness has always been fully satisfied within his triune being.

Twice in Matthew's Gospel—at Jesus' baptism and at the Transfiguration—we see extraordinary exhibitions of the triune God's happiness:

> When Jesus was baptized . . . behold, the heavens were opened to him, and he saw the Spirit of God descending like a dove and coming to rest on him; and behold, a voice from heaven said, "This is my beloved Son, with whom I am well pleased."
> MATTHEW 3:16-17

The Father, Son, and Holy Spirit all participate here, expressing pleasure and happiness in the Son.

At the Transfiguration, the Father's statement is repeated: "This is my beloved Son, with whom I am well pleased; listen to him" (Matthew 17:5). The Father says, "Behold my servant, whom I uphold, my chosen, in whom my soul delights" (Isaiah 42:1). For the Father to be well pleased and delighted with his Son means he finds great happiness in him.

Likewise, the Son and the Holy Spirit had every reason for total delight in one another and with the Father from before the dawn of time (see John 17:24; 1 Peter 1:20).

Steve DeWitt writes, "Before you ever had a happy moment,

or your great-grandparents had a happy moment, or Adam and Eve had a happy moment—before the universe was even created—God the Father and God the Son and God the Spirit were enjoying a perfect and robust relational delight in one another."[4]

God's communal happiness has significant implications for our own happiness. It means happiness didn't begin with the first human who experienced it. It also explains how God could be displeased with his creatures and their sin without disrupting his innate happiness.

Dick and Rick Hoyt, as father and son, delight in each other not just in triathlons but also in life. They are a beautiful reflection of God the Father and his Son. We are also called God's children, and just as Dick provides the strength Rick lacks, our Father provides the strength we lack. His happy love for us fuels our happy love for him.

———

Father, given our vast limitations, it's comforting to know that you don't depend on us—our actions, our affection, or our attitudes—for your happiness. You have your Son and your Spirit, and you have always enjoyed them. And, by a miracle of grace, you invite us to be your children and enter into your triune happiness. What could be a greater privilege?

Can God's creatures tap into his triune happiness?

From everlasting to everlasting you are God.   PSALM 90:2

Christians throughout the ages have said that by contemplating the Trinity they have found the ultimate essence, expression, and exercise of happiness.   JAMES HOUSTON

SINCE THE TRIUNE GOD had no beginning, neither did his happiness. Had God first experienced happiness at a particular point in time, we couldn't know whether his happiness would continue a million years from now. We would be left to wonder, *What if God was happy once and maybe still is, but one day he no longer will be?*

If we combine the doctrine of God's happiness with the doctrine of his immutability (his unchangeable nature), we'll understand that he must always remain happy. "Every good gift and every perfect gift is from above, coming down from the Father of lights with whom there is no variation or shadow due to change" (James 1:17). "Jesus Christ is the same yesterday and today and forever" (Hebrews 13:8).

Since God's nature doesn't change, we needn't fear that one day his happiness will wane or disappear. On the contrary, once sin, the enemy of happiness, is forever conquered, the happiness of God now evident in this world will expand exponentially and overwhelm us with its constant, pervasive brightness. When that day comes, we'll never need to try to be happy again—we'll be incapable of anything less.

God's happiness in us and our happiness in him are inseparable. We're all familiar with the question, *What do you give the person who has everything?* Who better fits that description than God? Yet we're told we can please God, delight him, and make him happy. God made us in his likeness. Doesn't it follow that just as I'm happy to give my wife, Nanci, my family, and my friends what makes them happy, so God is happy when his gifts make us happy?

I am convinced God makes his creatures happy and is made happy by their happiness. Think this through with me as I illustrate. I look out my kitchen window and watch our golden retriever, Maggie, play in the yard, her eyes wide and her nose to the ground, as if she expects something wonderful to appear. Then suddenly she stops and stares at something. It's a thick branch from a rhododendron she's been happily tearing to pieces.

Maggie pounces on this treasure, then marches around the yard with her prize, strutting like a conquering hero. If you asked me to describe my dog's state of mind, I would say, "Happy." From head to tail, she shows clear evidence that her delight is heartfelt.

When Nanci gets out Maggie's leash, it's a sight to behold. She gleefully runs in circles (Maggie, not Nanci—though Nanci is happy too). Maggie can't wait for her beloved owner to take her outside. During their walk, they enter into each other's joy, feeding off the happiness of the one they love.

As God sees us from Heaven, doesn't he delight in us the way Nanci and I delight in Maggie? The fact that God is infinitely smarter and greater than we are doesn't diminish his ability to find pleasure in us any more than our superior intelligence or worth interferes with our enjoyment of Maggie.

While there's a major difference between humans and animals, my dog and I have a common source for our happiness capacity: our Creator. God is the source of his own happiness and ours, and as his image bearers, both our capacity for happiness and our desire for it are modeled after his.

Scripture makes it plain that we are indwelt with two of the three persons of the Godhead, and by inference, we are indwelt with the third. This means that within us we have the triune God and his eternally joyous interrelationship. This is an astounding reality—we've been brought into an ancient and transcendent circle of happiness before and above all others. If we contemplated this truth daily, wouldn't it infuse our lives with wonder and delight?

We should recognize, welcome, and tap into that joy. It's

one thing to understand that God is happy. But as great a beginning as that is, believing in a happy God who is not distant but always with us and interested in our lives is better still. If we're convinced he is in us, enjoying the eternal happiness of his interrelationship in his triune self, this engages us in a circle of gladness that defies comprehension.

Jesus prayed, "I in them and you in me, that they may become perfectly one, so that the world may know that you sent me and loved them even as you loved me" (John 17:23). The Father, Son, and Holy Spirit are infinitely greater than we are, yet they share their love and happiness, enter into our happiness, and empower us to enter into theirs.

Who better than the triune God, who has always known happiness, to offer us, in him, the happiness we so deeply crave and could never experience on our own?

God, you who are Father, Son, and Holy Spirit, you are the source of all that is good and delightful, and all we need in order to be eternally happy. When we start chasing after things that won't last or bring us eternal happiness, remind us that all happiness comes from your hand. Where else but to you should we go to find it?

−DAY 36−

Is God's happiness confined to Heaven?

Well done, good and faithful servant! . . . Come and share your master's happiness! MATTHEW 25:23, NIV

The God of salvation, the God of the Covenant, is to be worshipped with joy! He is the happy God and He loves happy worshippers. CHARLES SPURGEON

NINETEENTH-CENTURY British preacher Charles Spurgeon faced many difficulties, including painful illnesses, his wife's immobility, and theological controversies. But nothing hurt him more deeply than what happened when he was preaching, as a twenty-two-year-old, to twelve thousand people. Someone yelled "Fire," though there was none. Seven people were trampled to death, and twenty-eight others were seriously injured. His closest friends said he never fully got over that tragedy. Spurgeon said, "Although my joy is greater than the most of men, my depression of spirit is such as few can have an idea of."[1]

But instead of listening to his depression, he listened to Scripture. Spurgeon wrote,

> *Because he lives, I shall live also, and I spring to my legs again and fight with my depressions of spirit and my down castings, and get the victory through it; and so may you do, and so you must, for there is no other way of escaping from it. In your most depressed seasons you are to get joy and peace through believing.*[2]

Norman Cousins gave an amazing account of the therapeutic value of laughter in his book *Anatomy of an Illness*.[3] Diagnosed with an untreatable terminal disease, his chance for recovery was one in five hundred.

Cousins believed that worry, depression, and anger had contributed to his illness. So he immersed himself in laughter, watching the Marx Brothers and other funny movies. He found that laughing for ten minutes relieved his pain for several hours. Eventually he made a full recovery and lived another twenty years. Cousins was convinced the laughter and his sustained focus on the bright side caused healing.

I find this story impossible to explain from a naturalistic worldview. Did this powerful, heart-energizing, body-healing thing called laughter come from random chemicals, protons, and neutrons? Can natural selection and survival of the fittest account for humor, laughter, and happiness?

Or are humor and laughter gifts to us? And if they're gifts, where could they originate but in God? And if God gives us the gifts of humor and laughter in this fallen world, what does it tell us about God himself?

Jonathan Edwards offered this succinct answer: "It is no defect in a fountain that it is prone to overflow."[4] God is a creator. But he doesn't create to be happy. Rather, he creates because he *is* happy. And that's what makes Heaven happy.

One of my Bible college professors often shared illustrations of Christ's presence in the small events of his day. As a student, I asked myself why those things didn't happen to me. As time passed, God showed me that in fact they did—I just hadn't noticed!

Since God is sovereign even in life's smallest events, shouldn't we think of leaves falling from trees, the rabbit bounding across a trail, the old friend we greet in the store, or the unexpected word of encouragement as further proof of God's happy and pleasure-giving nature?

Victor Hugo (1802–1885) wrote in *Les Misérables*, "The supreme happiness of life consists in the conviction that one is loved."[5] The greater the person who loves us, the greater our happiness. That's why every child of God should fixate on biblical promises such as, "No power in the sky above or in the earth below—indeed, nothing in all creation will ever be able to separate us from the love of God that is revealed in Christ Jesus our Lord" (Romans 8:39, NLT).

Though God grieves over the pain we experience here on Earth, he knows his perfect plan will prove best. He radiates love toward his children and patience toward the unsaved, yet he's angry at sin. He who was happy before the world began will be happy in the world to come, and he is happy now.

Our worldview is transformed when we realize that God wants us to share in his happiness—now and forever!

Nanci and I know the delight of sharing each other's happiness and that of our family and dear friends during vacations and reunions. Years later, those happy times still have the power to yield warm memories. But why should we think these wonderfully happy times are limited to our human relationships? If we believe Scripture, we can reverently seek to enjoy happiness and laughter with God himself.

I often remind myself that God is always with me. He wants us to know we can be happy both in him and with him—not only after we die, but as we live today. When I'm alone, whether I'm meditating or reading or looking at photos or watching a movie, any happiness or laughter I experience is a laugh I share with God because in fact, I am not alone!

John Bunyan (1628–1688), while imprisoned in the 1600s for preaching the gospel, wrote *The Pilgrim's Progress*—widely considered the most influential piece of literature other than the Bible. He said, "God is the chief good. . . . He is in himself most happy . . . and all true happiness is only to be found in God, as that which is essential to his nature."[6] To Bunyan, human happiness is inseparable from God and impossible unless God himself is happy. An unhappy God would never value nor assure the everlasting happiness of his creatures. We would never ask for grace from an ungracious God, kindness from an unkind God, or happiness from an unhappy God. It would be like asking a poor man for a million dollars. He can't give what he doesn't have.

If God were not happy, the fact that everyone seeks happiness would be a cruel tragedy, since it would mean that God cannot give us what we most deeply desire. At best he might deliver us from the miseries of Hell. But Heaven can overflow with happiness only if God himself overflows with happiness.

Our Creator's happiness guarantees a happy ending to the story that will never end.

Lord, we love that you are a happy Creator God! You give us hope for a future where you wipe away our tears and heal all our relationships, and where our laughter and joy will be as unending as yours. May we sense your happy presence with us here and now . . . even in the midst of life's greatest difficulties. Remind us that this is not the end of the story and that your blood-bought promise is to make all things right forever.

-DAY 37-

Is God's happiness a new thought?

I will greatly rejoice in the LORD; my soul shall exult in my God,
for he has clothed me with the garments of salvation.

ISAIAH 61:10

The beholding of God's happiness will increase the joy, to
consider that he is so happy who is so much the object of his
love. That love of God in those who shall see God, will cause
them exceedingly to rejoice in the happiness of God.

JONATHAN EDWARDS

IN HIS BOOK *IS GOD HAPPY?*, Marxist philosopher Leszek
Kołakowski answers no to his title question. He says that God
can't be happy and that as long as there's pain and death,
humans can't be happy either. If happiness were utterly incompatible with sin and sorrow, I'd have to agree. But despite
present conditions in the universe, God's unchanging nature
includes underlying happiness—and the power to give us reasons for happiness too.

Though a long line of ancient philosophers, theologians,

161

and regular folks once believed in God's happiness, this concept has largely disappeared from the thoughts of countless Christians. It's time to rediscover what believers before us knew and taught for centuries.

Anselm was a Benedictine monk who became the archbishop of Canterbury. Arguably, he was the greatest theologian between Augustine and Aquinas. In the opening of his philosophical treatise *Monologion*, Anselm spoke of the things "we must believe about God." One of those was God's happiness: "There is one nature, supreme among all existing things, who alone is self-sufficient in his eternal happiness, who through his omnipotent goodness grants and brings it about."[1] Few of us would be surprised that Anselm included God's omnipotence and goodness, but most modern Christians tend to bypass God's happiness.

Puritan Matthew Henry (1662–1714), the greatest Bible commentator of his era, wrote, "The eternal God, though infinitely happy in the enjoyment of himself, yet took a satisfaction in the work of his own hands."[2] God was all-happy before Creation, yet he delighted in his creation in a special way.

John Gill (1697–1771) sang God's praise in ways that may seem surprising for a "body of divinity" written by a Hebrew scholar, pastor, and serious theologian:

> *Happy, thrice happy, are the people whose God is the*
> *Lord! Who, besides the good things he bestows on them*

*here, he has laid up such goodness for them hereafter,
which the heart of man cannot conceive of. How blessed
and happy then must he himself be! Name whatsoever
it may be thought happiness consists in, and it will be
found in God in its full perfection.*[3]

H. D. M. Spence-Jones (1836–1917) was a Cambridge gradu-
ate who taught Hebrew and was the general editor of *The Pulpit
Commentary*. I was struck by his observation on Jeremiah
32:41, where God says, "I will rejoice in doing them good, and
I will plant them in this land in faithfulness, with all my heart
and all my soul."

Spence-Jones wrote,

*God has joy. He is not indifferent, nor is he morose;
we are to think of him as the "blessed" God, i.e. as
essentially happy. . . . The brightness and beauty of
the world are reflections from the blessedness of God.
Because he is glad, nature is glad, flowers bloom, birds
sing, young creatures bound with delight. Nothing
is more sad in perversions of religion than the
representations of God as a gloomy tyrant. . . .*

*These fragrant meadows, broad rolling seas of
moorland heather, rich green forest-cities of busy insect
life, flashing ocean waves, and the pure blue sky above,
and all that is sweet and lovely in creation, swell one*

symphony of gladness, because the mighty Spirit that haunts them is himself overflowing with joy. Our God is a Sun. And if divinity is sunny, so should religion be. The happy God will rejoice in the happiness of his children. . . . God is so joyous that he finds joy even in us.[4]

Modern writer John McReynolds says, "God is happy. His happiness is an intrinsic part of who He is. He was happy in eternity past, He is happy now, and He will be happy for all eternity. . . . His happiness, like all of His other attributes, is infinite and absolute."[5]

May we today, in our own lives and families and churches, add our names to the list of Christ-followers throughout the ages who believed that God is happy, that Jesus his Son is happy, and that the gospel we believe and embrace and share with others is a happy one.

Father, help us to grasp the liberating, gladness-producing truth of your happiness. Knowing that you are so happy that your delight spills out in the universe and in us changes everything—now and forever. Empower us to live this day in the awareness of this great truth.

Why were so many people attracted to Jesus?

I have told you this to make you as completely happy as I am.
JESUS (JOHN 15:11, CEV)

The best work is done by the happy, joyful workman. And so it is with Christ. He does not save souls as of necessity—as though He would rather do something else if He might—but His very heart is in it, He rejoices to do it, and therefore He does it thoroughly and He communicates His joy to us in the doing of it. CHARLES SPURGEON

MY WIFE LED a women's Bible study group in discussing a lesson she'd written about the happiness of Jesus. One woman who'd grown up a churchgoer was startled. She shared how horrified she'd been once to see a picture of Jesus smiling. Why? Because she believed it was blasphemous to make Jesus appear happy!

Actor Bruce Marchiano, who played Jesus in a movie based on Matthew's Gospel, received this remarkable letter:

A few weeks ago I was halfway watching TV and happened to look up, and there was "Jesus" (you) walking along the banks of the Sea of Galilee. . . . He slowly looked over His shoulder, smiled a big smile, and motioned to follow Him. My heart leaped right out of my chest! . . . It was Jesus like I'd never considered Him to be, and in a moment I was convinced in my heart that Jesus just had to be this way—completely different from everything I'd ever thought! Glowing with excitement from His face— from His eyes. A strong, energetic, passionate, joyous man! It instantaneously transformed my relationship with Him—so much so, I grieve to think of all the decades I've wasted knowing Him, but not knowing Him; loving Him and receiving His love from some distant place, but never being "in love" with Him. Well . . . I am now![1]

When believers demonstrate genuine happiness, it draws people to God and the gospel. A young woman tells her story about coming to know Jesus:

Before I met him my life was going down the drain. I had nothing to live for, let alone die for. There was no light at the end of my tunnel. In fact, there wasn't even a tunnel. Only a deep, damp grave. Those days passed long ago, but I can't ever let myself forget them. . . .

I had never been in a church my whole life and I was

unsure about what I should do. My heart began to panic. As we took our seats I relaxed a little. . . . I also noticed everyone's faces were so lit up with happy expressions. I never knew church made people happy.

After the service . . . I wanted to go back again and again and find out what all the happiness was about. I soon learned that it wasn't the church that made people happy, but rather, it was God and his son Jesus. They were the reason for the happy expressions on people's faces.[2]

Countless believers have similar stories. People are attracted to Jesus when they see his attributes in others' lives. They've observed kindness, graciousness, and happiness, and as a result, they want to know the source of those qualities.

I didn't meet a lot of "cool" people in the church where I first heard the gospel. And while there were some church curmudgeons (there always are), I met a number of regular Christ-loving people who displayed profound peace, contentment, warmth, and happiness. When I saw these qualities, I couldn't ignore them. These were characteristics I admired and wanted. They drew me toward the Christ these people worshiped. And when I came to know Jesus myself, the happiness I found in him was deeper than I'd ever dreamed.

Have you ever thought about the eternally happy Son of God enjoying happiness as a human being for the first time? I have to believe that his smiles, his laughter, and the words he spoke to his Father were full of delight as he marveled at his incarnation, which, because of his resurrection, will never end!

A. W. Tozer wrote, "[God] meant us to see Him and live with Him and draw our life from His smile."[3] The smile of Jesus is not like the smile of Buddha—disconnected from suffering. Jesus smiles as one who, having been happy from eternity past and fully knowing the cost, chose to take on the worst suffering imaginable to secure our everlasting happiness. We view Jesus as the deity who miraculously puts an end to all suffering—and so he will—but meanwhile we need to see him as the one who understands and experiences both joy and suffering, and is committed to using both for his glory.

A wise person once observed, "The early Christians did not say in dismay, 'look what the world has come to,' but in delight, 'look what has come into the world.'"[4]

"What has come" is Jesus Christ—a person so attractive, so magnetic, and so joyful that he changed the world not only by his death but also by the quality of his life.

———

Jesus, we want people to know you and to join us in the happiness we enjoy through you. Please help us to make the best of every opportunity, first to experience happiness in you and then to show our happiness, always giving you the credit. Your love is contagious. Help us spread it everywhere we go.

-DAY 39-

Is Jesus happy?

For the joy that was set before him [Christ] endured the cross, despising the shame, and is seated at the right hand of the throne of God. HEBREWS 12:2

In Christ one sees the path to happiness and discovers the virtues and practices constitutive of happiness. For Christians, happiness is a way of life by which we gradually are conformed to the love, goodness, and beauty of God revealed to us in Christ. PAUL WADELL

MANY SCHOLARS BELIEVE that Christ is the personification of "Lady Wisdom," who is depicted in Proverbs 8. Speaking of the Father, this ancient and eternal Wisdom says, "When he established the heavens, I was there. . . . When he marked out the foundations of the earth, then I was beside him, like a master workman" (verses 27, 29-30). Wisdom—clearly not just an attribute, but a being—says, "I was constantly at his side. I was filled with delight day after day, rejoicing always in his presence, rejoicing in his whole world and delighting in mankind" (verses 30-31, NIV).

Dylan Demarsico says of this passage, "Rejoicing is a conservative translation of the Hebrew word *sachaq*. More accurate would be *laughing* or *playing*. We're understandably reluctant to ascribe *laughing* and *playing* to Almighty God. Still, you can see for yourself in any Hebrew lexicon what the word means—and subsequently what God and wisdom were doing when they created the world: laughing and playing."[1]

The Common English Bible captures these words of God's all-wise Son: "I was having fun, *smiling* before him all the time, *frolicking* with his inhabited earth and delighting in the human race" (Proverbs 8:30-31, emphasis added). The Good News Translation says, "I was his daily source of joy, always happy in his presence—happy with the world and pleased with the human race."

Creation is attributed to Christ (see John 1:1-3; Colossians 1:16). But here he's seen as playfully interacting with his Father and his creation. What an amazing portrayal of the preincarnate happiness of Jesus!

Demarsico says of this passage, "If you had witnessed this transcendent Being-in-Three-Persons letting out roaring laughter as he played, thus creating the universe, you probably would have shouted and cried out with joy. . . . The joy of the Lord is not something trifling. It's a playfulness that created and sustains the universe, a laughter that guides history to its glorious end."[2]

Since we're told that the angels shouted for joy when the triune God created Earth (see Job 38:4, 7), surely we would have done the same. Perhaps we will someday on the New Earth—maybe God will open the past and delight us with a front-row seat beholding his original creation!

In the first-ever gospel message of the newborn church, the apostle Peter preached that Psalm 16 is about Christ: "David says concerning him, 'I saw the Lord always before me, for he is at my right hand that I may not be shaken; therefore my heart was *glad*, and my tongue *rejoiced*. . . . For you will not abandon my soul to Hades, or let your Holy One see corruption. . . . You will make me *full of gladness* with your presence'" (Acts 2:25-28, emphasis added). This effusive statement, attributed to the Messiah, is a triple affirmation of his happiness!

The passage Peter ascribed to Jesus includes Psalm 16:11: "In your presence there is fullness of joy; at your right hand are pleasures forevermore." The New Life Version says, "Being with You is to be full of joy. In Your right hand there is happiness forever."

I'm convinced we should view this first apostolic sermon as a model for sharing the gospel today. Peter, full of the Holy Spirit, preached a prototypical gospel message, asserting three times the happiness of the one who is at the center of the gospel—Jesus. Yet how many people, unbelievers and believers alike, have ever heard a modern gospel message that makes this point? Peter preached that Jesus was "full of gladness"; why shouldn't we?

Psalm 45:6-7 is quoted in direct reference to the Messiah in Hebrews 1:8-9, where the Father says of his Son, "You have loved righteousness and hated wickedness; therefore God, your God, has anointed you with the oil of gladness beyond your companions." The Contemporary English Version renders it, "Your God . . . made you happier than any of your friends."

Who are Jesus' companions in this passage? This could refer to his immediate group of friends, all believers, or all his fellow human beings. If it's the latter, he has gladness that exceeds that of all people (which makes sense because he created us). If we were to ask a random group of believers and unbelievers, "Who is the happiest human being who ever lived?" few people would give the correct answer: "Jesus."

Reflecting on these passages in Psalm 45 and Hebrews 1, John Piper writes, "Jesus Christ is the happiest being in the universe. His gladness is greater than all the angelic gladness of heaven. He mirrors perfectly the infinite, holy, indomitable mirth of his Father."[3]

Lord Jesus, your happiness is a gift you share with our Father and the Holy Spirit, and—miraculously, inexplicably, extravagantly—with us! Thank you!

Did Jesus have a sense of humor?

You blind guides, straining out a gnat and swallowing a camel!
JESUS (MATTHEW 23:24)

If there is a single person within the pages of the Bible that we can consider to be a humorist, it is without doubt Jesus.
DICTIONARY OF BIBLICAL IMAGERY

A FRIEND AND I SPENT three hours at lunch with Carol King, a godly woman in her fifties who was dying of cancer. She'd read a few of my books and wanted to talk about Heaven. What struck me as we spent time sharing together was an unexpected gift—the gift of laughter.

"I need new clothes," Carol said, "but why buy them? I used to get jumbo-sized shampoo, but now I get small bottles. I don't even buy green bananas, because by the time they ripen I'll probably be gone!" Carol laughed as she spoke. It wasn't a morbid or cynical laugh, but one that naturally flowed from heartfelt peace. She anticipated being with Jesus in a better world. She'd already suffered great pain and had no romantic notions about death. Yet she faced the end of her time on Earth with quiet joy and Christ-honoring laughter that invited us to laugh as much as she did.

Nanci and I find that lightheartedness and humor is our release, our safety valve during tough times. Laughter is therapeutic. It heals. It gives hope and vitality.

Did Satan create laughter? Was it fashioned by humans? No. Scripture says of God, "He will yet fill your mouth with laughter, and your lips with shouts of joy" (Job 8:21, NRSV).

People often reject the idea of Jesus being happy by quoting from Isaiah 53:3: "He was despised and rejected by men; a man of sorrows, and acquainted with grief." But the context shows that he's called "a man of sorrows" not in general, but specifically in relationship to his suffering and sacrificial work. Going to the cross, Jesus said, "My soul is deeply grieved to the point of death" (Mark 14:34, NASB).

But he lived more than twelve thousand days, and this was the worst twenty-four hours of his life. Given the price he paid for our sins, does being "a man of sorrows" in his atoning work contradict the notion Jesus was happy? Absolutely not. Sorrow and happiness can and do coexist within the same person.

Jesus understood that the basis for his sorrow was temporary, while the basis for his gladness was and is permanent. He'd known unbounded happiness before the dawn of time, and he knew it awaited him again.

Scripture says of Jesus, "By him all things were created" (Colossians 1:16). Laughter comes from the Creator, who made us in his image! God's laughter preceded our own laughter and is the ongoing source of it. We can be happy only because he's happy; we can laugh because he laughs.

Jesus says, "How happy are you who weep now, for you are going to laugh!" (Luke 6:21, PHILLIPS). In context, he's talking about people having great reward in Heaven. In other words, he's saying, "You will laugh in Heaven." Surely Jesus will join in the laughter—and when he laughs, it's always the laughter of both God and man.

Jesus goes on to say, "Woe to you who laugh now, for you shall mourn and weep" (Luke 6:25). The laughter he opposes is laughter at injustice, immorality, and other things that dishonor God. Obviously, laughter can be twisted by sin, just as eating and drinking can.

As believers, we need to laugh a great deal more and a great deal less: more at ourselves and the incongruities of life, and less at immorality and mockery of what pleases God.

We don't have depictions of the disciples sitting around campfires telling stories or teasing each other. But I'm certain they did, because that's what people do. Did Jesus joke with his friends? The better question is, Why wouldn't he? Jesus knew what Solomon did: there is "a time to weep, and a time to laugh; a time to mourn, and a time to dance" (Ecclesiastes 3:4). Surely we should believe he did all of these!

Growing up in a faithful Jewish family, Jesus would have enjoyed many feasts and holidays, as well as the weekly Sabbath, all celebratory experiences (see chapter 33 of my book *Happiness*). One of the psalms that Jesus would have meditated on from his childhood says, "When the LORD brought us back to Jerusalem, it was like a dream! How we laughed, how we sang for joy! . . . Indeed he did great things for us; how happy we were!"(Psalm 126:1-3, GNT).

Laughter is not only human, it's explicitly biblical and pleasing to God. It's therefore inconceivable that Jesus didn't laugh! Did humor come into the universe as the result of sin? No. We have a sense of humor because as his image bearers, we're similar to God, who enjoys laughter.

The humor of Jesus is far more apparent if we understand his culture and engaging personality. There's nothing disrespectful about noticing that many of Jesus' statements are, by design, happily outrageous.

Jesus told the religious leaders they were sightless, missing the whole point of following God: "You blind guides, straining out a gnat and swallowing a camel!" (Matthew 23:24). Straining out a gnat would have been hard work for anyone— but impossible for the blind. And what could be more ridiculous than swallowing a camel? This odd and pithy statement undoubtedly caused laughter to erupt.

Jesus may have laughed at some of the limitations of his own humanity. He didn't sin or make foolish decisions, but did he ever fall down, spill milk, or hit his thumb while hammering? He who made the heavens with his fingers (see Psalm 8:3) surely got splinters in them while working with wood all day. I doubt he complained, but I do think he marveled at what it means to be human. Remember, Jesus brought into the world not only the grace and truth of God but also the happiness, delight, humor, and laughter of God.

One day in the presence of Jesus, we'll know what it means to have entered our Master's happiness. And on the New Earth, as we play and feast and joke and tell stories together, always looking to the one who redeemed us, I truly believe that no laugh will be louder, and no happiness larger, than his.

Jesus, thank you for creating laughter and setting the perfect example of how to enjoy humor. What a wonderful way to bring us healing. What a gift from your loving hand! Open our eyes to the delights around us and help us enjoy the kind of laughter and humor that honors you.

Can happiness really be spiritual?

*Let all those who seek You rejoice and be glad in You; and
let those who love Your salvation say continually, "Let God
be magnified!"* PSALM 70:4, NKJV

*Living for others is really the Christ life after all. Oh,
the satisfaction, happiness and joy one gets out of it.*
GEORGE WASHINGTON CARVER

JOY CAN BE SPIRITUAL or unspiritual, as can happiness.
Isaac Watts (1674–1748), who wrote "Joy to the World," also
spoke of "carnal joys."[1]

Charles Spurgeon recognized the difference between false
and true joy:

*Christ would not have us rejoice with the false joy of
presumption, so He bares the sharp knife and cuts that
joy away. Joy on a false basis would prevent us from
having true joy, and therefore . . . the joy we may get*

*may be worth having—not the mere surf and foam of
a wave that is driven with the wind and tossed, but
the solid foundation of the Rock of Ages!*[2]

Someone can have Christ-centered happiness or Christ-denying happiness. The former will last forever; the latter has an exceedingly short shelf life.

Notice A. W. Tozer's negative use of *joy* and positive use of *happiness* more than sixty years ago: "Human beings are busy trying to work up a joy of some sort. They try it in dance halls . . . they turn to television programs. But we still don't see the truly happy faces."[3] Tozer realized that artificial attempts at creating joy can't create the happiness that only comes from Christ.

When God calls us to rejoice in him, does he care only about what we think and do, not how we *feel* about him? No. He commands us to love him, not just with all our minds but with all our *hearts* (see Matthew 22:37).

In a remarkable passage, God rebukes people not for failing to serve him but for serving him unhappily: "Because you did not serve the Lord your God joyfully and gladly in the time of prosperity, therefore in hunger and thirst, in nakedness and dire poverty, you will serve the enemies the Lord sends against you" (Deuteronomy 28:47-48, NIV).

Yes, it's possible to obey and serve God without feeling joy. But God emphatically says he wants us to feel joy! Feelings are not the entirety of joy, but since God's joy involves emotions, shouldn't our joy involve emotions?

The psalmist said, "I will go to the altar of God, to God my exceeding joy, and I will praise you with the lyre, O God, my God" (Psalm 43:4). Can you imagine saying to someone, "You are my exceeding joy" without feeling strong emotion?

Mike Mason writes,

> *When I'm joyful, I'm happy, and when I'm happy, I'm joyful. What could be plainer? Why should I want anything to do with a joy that isn't coupled with happiness, or with a kind of happiness that is without joy? Happiness without joy is shallow and transient because it's based on outward circumstances rather than an attitude of the heart. As for joy without happiness, it's a spiritualized lie. The Bible does not separate joy and happiness and neither should we.*[4]

David Murray identifies six kinds of happiness available to unbelievers and believers alike:

- *nature happiness*
- *social happiness*
- *vocational happiness*
- *physical happiness*

- *intellectual happiness*
- *humor happiness*

The one remaining component, available only to believers, is spiritual happiness. Murray calls it "a joy that at times contains more pleasure and delight than the other six put together."[5]

Spiritual happiness comes in contemplating God and drawing close to him. Of course, the other six aren't "unspiritual" forms of happiness. Because they're God given, they're spiritual, though not redemptive. But without the seventh kind of happiness, the first six are temporary. A reconciled relationship with God, in concert with an understanding of the biblical teaching of a resurrected Heaven and Earth, assures us that all happiness will be ours forever.

Jesus experienced all forms of happiness, and so can we. With an eternal perspective, only the righteous enjoy true happiness (see Psalm 16:11; 21:6; 36:7-10; 37:16; 43:4; 73:28; John 10:10). The forever that awaits us should color our lives now. We should daily front-load eternity's joys into our present experience.

Spurgeon said it well:

Are there not periods of life when we feel so glad that we would fain dance for joy? Let not such exhilaration be spent upon common themes, but let the name of God stir us to ecstasy. . . . There is enough in our holy faith to create and to justify the utmost degree of rapturous delight. If men are dull in the worship of the Lord our God they are not acting consistently with the character of their religion.[6]

———

Father, your kindness and grace are hard to understand but easy to appreciate. Thank you for the joy you've brought into our world through the gift of your Son. May those who have tasted happiness and joy but do not know you be drawn to the Christ-centered joy of your people. Help us to realize how eager you are to infuse our hearts with your happiness. Move us not only to serve you but also to serve you joyfully and gladly, thereby bringing you joy and gladness.

-DAY 42-

What role do our attitudes play in our happiness?

I concluded there is nothing better than to be happy and enjoy ourselves as long as we can.   ECCLESIASTES 3:12, NLT

There is no automatic joy. Christ is not a happiness capsule; he is the way to the Father. But the way to the Father is not a carnival ride in which we sit and do nothing while we are whisked through various spiritual sensations.

CALVIN MILLER

ONCE UPON A TIME, a widow had two sons who provided for her. One sold umbrellas and the other, fans. Every morning the mother checked the weather. Sunshine brought her misery, because no umbrellas would sell. Rain brought her misery, because no fans would sell. Both conditions caused her to fret.

One day her friend remarked, "If the sun is shining, people buy fans. If it rains, they buy umbrellas. Change your attitude; be happy!"

It's a simple story, but it illustrates a potentially life-changing reality. Our happiness is dependent not on circumstances but on perspective. The Greek philosopher Epictetus said, "Men are disturbed not by the things which happen, but by the opinions about the things."[1]

At nineteen months old, Helen Keller (1880–1968) contracted an illness that left her deaf and blind. Alexander Graham Bell, who worked with deaf children, advised her parents to contact Boston's Perkins Institute for the Blind, and as a result, former student Anne Sullivan became Keller's instructor.

Keller took advantage of the training with her teacher and began to learn at an astonishing rate. Everything hinged on her attitude and perspective. She wrote, "When one door of happiness closes, another opens; but often we look so long at the closed door that we do not see the one which has been opened for us."[2] She looked for open doors instead of obsessing about closed ones.

Even if many doors around us have closed, don't most of us have more open doors than Keller did? We're inspired by stories of those who rise above their difficulties and live happy and productive lives. Why shouldn't we ourselves live out the kind of story that will inspire others and leave us content and fulfilled? Our perspectives and attitudes as we call upon God for his grace and his joy will prove to be the keys to such a story.

David Brainerd (1718–1747) served as a missionary to the Delaware Indians of New Jersey. He was orphaned at fourteen, and in college he suffered from debilitating tuberculosis. Having endured great suffering while serving in a fruitful ministry, he died at age twenty-nine. His biography inspired many, including pioneer missionary William Carey as well as missionary martyr Jim Elliot. During Brainerd's final illness, he was nursed by Jonathan Edwards's daughter Jerusha, who may have contracted tuberculosis from him. She died four months after he did. Depressing story, right? But in fact, the story involved much happiness.

Understandably, Brainerd's diary frequently references his pain, using the word 78 times and *suffer* or *suffering* 30 times. Yet the most striking thing about his writing is how many more references he makes to his happiness in God and others: he uses *happy* and *happiness* 60 times, *delight* 50 times, *pleased* and *pleasure* 177 times, *joy* and *enjoy* 350 times. He also uses *blessed* more than 200 times, often meaning "happy."

Though his life was not typical, like all of us Brainerd experienced both sorrow and joy: "This morning the Lord was pleased to lift up the light of His countenance upon me. . . . Though I have been so depressed of late, respecting my hopes of future serviceableness in the cause of God, yet now I had much encouragement. . . . I felt exceedingly calm and quite resigned to God, respecting my future employment. . . . My faith lifted me above the world and removed all those mountains that I could not look over."[3]

On his twenty-fourth birthday, racked with pain, Brainerd wrote, "This has been a sweet, a happy day to me."[4]

Honesty about his illness and periodic depression demonstrated Brainerd's sincerity about his happiness. He wrote, "It appeared such a happiness to have God for my portion that I had rather be any other creature in this lower creation than not come to the enjoyment of God. . . . Lord, endear Thyself more to me!"[5]

Brainerd spoke of "the absolute dependence of a creature upon God the Creator, for every crumb of happiness it enjoys."[6] He said of God, "He is the supreme good, the only soul-satisfying happiness."[7]

One painful day he "found some relief in prayer; loved, as a feeble, afflicted, despised creature, to cast myself on a God of infinite grace and goodness, hoping for no happiness but from Him. . . . Toward night, I felt my soul rejoice that God is unchangeably happy and glorious."[8]

A terribly sick young man was able to rejoice that God is, always has been, and always will be happy! How many Christians today, in times of suffering, take such solace in the happiness of God?

Brainerd made the daily choice to meditate on God, see him all around, listen to his Word and God's people, and behold him in his creation. He looked for happiness in God. He wrote,

"If you hope for happiness *in* the world, hope for it from God, and not *from* the world."[9]

If a young man without modern medicine and dying of an excruciating disease could make choices that brought him happiness in Christ, surely we can too.

———

Lord Jesus, *when we look to you as our spring and source, we can choose to tap into happiness. Who could look at you and not be happy? Who would want to look at anyone or anything less? Thank you for David Brainerd's example of seeking and finding genuine happiness in you, despite life's difficulties. Help us remember whose we are. We love you, our King. Thanks for being the dearest friend we could ever have and for remaining our friend forever!*

-DAY 43-

How do our actions affect our happiness?

[Jesus'] divine power has granted to us all things that pertain to life and godliness, through the knowledge of him who called us to his own glory and excellence, by which he has granted to us his precious and very great promises, so that through them you may become partakers of the divine nature. 2 PETER 1:3-4

Research has proven that if you want to be happy . . . serve others. People who volunteer and give become happier as a result, because the key to happiness is to labor for the happiness of others. . . . Those who feel happy are also more productive, effective and successful. ARTHUR BROOKS

WHAT DO GOD'S CHILDREN lack in order to live godly, happy lives? Absolutely nothing. We're told God's power has "granted to us all things that pertain to life and godliness." All we need has already been granted to us, along with "his precious and very great promises," which enable us, through his Holy Spirit, to access God's own nature, including his happiness.

188

If you believe in the God of the Bible, if you've placed your faith in Jesus Christ as your Redeemer, then the following things are true:

- *The price for your happiness has been paid.*
- *The basis for your happiness is secure.*
- *The resources for your happiness are provided daily.*
- *The assurance of your eternal happiness is absolute, providing an objective reason for your happiness today.*

To better know, follow, worship, and love Christ *produces happiness in Christ.* We can't skip these steps in order to get to happiness. It doesn't work that way. We must choose to meditate and build daily upon the foundations of our happiness, not wait for happiness to magically arrive.

Happiness researchers have found that circumstances can contribute about 10 percent to our happiness—a remarkably small percentage. Next comes our internal makeup, including genetic factors and temperament, which can account for 50 percent of our happiness level.[1] The final 40 percent, the experts say, is entirely within our control: our choices, behaviors, and thoughts.[2]

We're commanded in Scripture, "Do not be conformed to this world, but be transformed by the renewal of your mind" (Romans 12:2). This change in thinking is our responsibility. German Reformer Martin Luther (1483–1546) is credited with saying, "You can't stop the birds from flying over your head, but you can keep them from making a nest in your hair." We choose thoughts that lead us either toward or away from Christ, and therefore toward or away from happiness in Christ.

Yes, we can learn to control our thoughts. They're not foreign invaders against which we have no defense.

Since God is sovereign over circumstances, genetics, background, and temperaments, even the 60 percent of happiness factors secular research affirms we can't change are used by God to accomplish his purpose. And the 40 percent under our control are subject to the Holy Spirit's influence.

Sometimes small, easy choices bring happiness—flipping through a photo album, riding a horse, baking cookies, or dining out. Today I played about a dozen popular songs Nanci and I grew up with, and we smiled the whole time.

Other times life involves such sadness and stress that we must go through multiple steps and the passing of time—with moments of laughter along the way—before a settled joy can emerge. David began a psalm with these words: "Be gracious to me, O LORD, for I am languishing; heal me, O LORD, for my bones are troubled. . . . I am weary with my moaning; every night I flood my bed with tears" (Psalm 6:2, 6). Near the end of the psalm, he says, "The LORD has heard the sound of my weeping. The LORD has heard my plea; the LORD accepts my prayer" (verses 8-9). This realization lays the groundwork for moving David toward the kind of powerful joy that is so evident in other psalms. Sometimes we move quickly to happiness, other times more gradually.

Both modern research and Scripture put the ball in our court. Happy people give generously, serve others, and seek to make others happy. Happiness doesn't precede giving and serving; it accompanies and follows it. Those who sit around waiting to be happy shouldn't hold their breath—it will likely be a long wait!

A 2010 survey revealed that of 4,500 Americans who volunteered an average of one hundred hours a year, 68 percent reported feeling physically healthier, 73 percent said volunteering "lowered my stress levels," and 89 percent reported that it "has improved my sense of well-being."[3] This idea that happiness requires action isn't controversial. Research corresponds perfectly with Scripture. Speaking of our spiritual gifts, Paul said, "Let us use them. . . . The one who does acts of mercy, with cheerfulness" (Romans 12:6, 8). We're not just told to be cheerful but to use our gifts cheerfully, which spreads joy to others.

As a young pastor, I led our church's counseling ministry. I said to various married couples, "You meet with me and then have the illusion that you did something to help your marriage—but coming here means nothing unless you actually make the changes we talk about." When it comes to happiness, the same principle applies: speaking or reading about it doesn't necessarily make it happen.

I've heard people talk about their hopes or plans to one day read the Bible regularly, give generously, volunteer for children's ministry, or go on a mission trip. God's gift of happiness isn't based on what we'd like to do or hope to do or even plan to do—only on what we actually *do*.

Simply recognizing that happiness comes from knowing, loving, and serving God is a good beginning, but it isn't enough. We need to open God's Word, go to the Bible study, join a church, volunteer at a homeless shelter, write a check to support Bible translation for unreached people groups, or go on a summer mission trip. If we want new and better results when it comes to our happiness, we must *act*!

Father, we need your empowerment to make choices that will enlarge our happiness in you. Help us seek to be happy in you by meditating on your Word and making the most of every opportunity to give our lives for you and others. By a work of your grace, grant us the courage and conviction to act on the opportunities you faithfully provide.

-DAY 44-

Why not make happiness a habit?

In everything by prayer and supplication with thanksgiving let your requests be made known to God. And the peace of God, which surpasses all understanding, will guard your hearts and your minds in Christ Jesus.   PHILIPPIANS 4:6-7

You more likely act yourself into feeling than feel yourself into action.   JEROME BRUNER

THE DAILY EXPERIENCE OF happiness requires our sustained effort. When Nanci and I bought our house nearly forty years ago, it didn't become ours in any meaningful sense until we took possession. Likewise, our happiness was bought and paid for by Christ. But until we actually take hold of it, it's not really ours. To find happiness we must move into it.

Scripture repeatedly shows that when we come to Christ, we are no longer in bondage to sin (see Romans 6:18). Yes, we still can and do sin, but in any given moment we don't have to—we have a new nature in Christ and the enablement of the

Spirit (see 2 Corinthians 5:17). However, God doesn't force us to obey him; he gives us a choice.

Consider Philippians 2:12-13: "Work out your own salvation with fear and trembling [our actions], for it is God who works in you [God's actions], both to will and to work for his good pleasure [God's actions]." We don't have to choose between God's sovereignty and human will; this passage teaches participation by both parties. This partnership occurs when two beings genuinely work together, without any implication of equality in intellect, authority, or resolve. (Naturally, any partnership between the infinite Creator God and finite, fallen human beings is decidedly unequal!)

We can't make ourselves happy in God any more than a seed can make itself grow. But we're not just seeds. We're greenhouse farmers who can make sure the seed is planted, watered, and fertilized.

Paul said to the church in Corinth, "I planted, Apollos watered, but God gave the growth" (1 Corinthians 3:6). While God makes the crop grow, the people who raise the largest and best produce, winning ribbons at the county fair, do their part too.

It's not always easy to choose what brings ultimate, lasting happiness over what brings instant, temporary happiness. Choosing happiness is not merely working harder to pull up our minds and moods, as we would our bootstraps. Rather, it's gratefully receiving God's grace and happiness.

Still, there's a lot to be said for "Just do it." Too many of us wait for sufficient motivation before making wise and joy-producing choices. But whether it's exercise, eating right, or volunteering to serve others, when we take those first steps, we overcome inertia and establish new habits. Once we see the positive happiness that results, we're much more motivated to keep up those new patterns.

When a physical action is repeated over time, long-term muscle memory is formed. Climbing, typing, and playing musical instruments all utilize muscle memory. This is similar to how happiness works: the brain has its own muscle memory. We choose to follow Christ by taking a certain action, we find happiness in it, and then we do it again because of the payoff we receive. When we turn off the television and read a good book, we feel better—more engaged and enriched. Recalling that, we do the same thing again, and eventually it becomes a habit. We end up reading not just because we think we should but because we want to.

Both happiness and unhappiness are states of mind that self-perpetuate. The more delighted we are, the more delight becomes our default. The angrier we are, the more anger becomes our default.

Paul said, "Fix your thoughts on what is true. . . . Think about things that are excellent and worthy of praise" (Philippians 4:8, NLT). This doesn't happen automatically. But once we develop the habit and experience its rewards, we instinctively turn our minds to what makes us happy in Christ.

Everyone who has dieted knows that nearly any diet works when habitually followed, but no diet works when repeatedly violated. It's not the inherent virtue of a diet or exercise plan but the daily choices related to diet or exercise that determine results.

Some believers become obsessed with everything that's wrong with the world. We're continually bombarded by "news" (which is sometimes more sensational than informative) that dwells on the sufferings and tragedies of life. It's easy for the unceasing avalanche of bad news to bury the Good News. I don't favor living in a cave, blissfully ignorant of the world's woes. But we are to focus our thoughts on true eternal realities by remembering God's presence, praying, and feeding our minds with good things that honor our King.

When I'm snorkeling for hours on end, taking underwater photos, I don't think about being cold, hungry, or tired—not because I'm in denial, but because I'm so focused on the magnificent and praiseworthy creativity of my God, who made the ocean's wonders.

When I was a young boy, I collected rocks. There were lots of plain stones, as well as muddy ones, with worms and bugs all around and under them. But this didn't deter me, because I wasn't collecting worms or bugs; I was collecting beautiful stones. Even when they didn't appear beautiful, I saw their hidden beauty.

Why not make happiness a habit?

As I collected rocks, and as others collect coins and stamps, we can collect reasons to praise God. We can develop an eye for beauty in God, his world, and the people and man-made objects in it. That's not denying the Curse; it's cultivating the happiness of a God-centered worldview.

Even in a fallen world, God invites us to happiness in him. Why would we say no, when all it takes to say yes is making small decisions that produce large results?

———

Dear Jesus, please remind us to be active, not passive, when it comes to seeking Christ-honoring happiness. Help us develop new disciplines that will unlock more of your happiness in our lives. May we fix our minds on what's pleasing to you—things that are honorable, just, pure, lovely, commendable, excellent, and worthy of praise. Always and above all, move us to fix our minds on you, the endlessly deep well of all that is good and delightful.

-DAY 45-

What can we do to cultivate happiness?

Let me hear the sounds of joy and gladness; and though you have crushed me and broken me, I will be happy once again.

PSALM 51:8, GNT

Do you want a happy heart when you are old? Then get with the Lord and stay with Him. That is how it works.

SHELTON SMITH

STELLA'S FIRST CHRISTMAS as a widow brought incredible loneliness. One day her doorbell rang and she was greeted by a messenger holding a box.

"What's in the box?" she asked.

The messenger opened the flap to reveal a Labrador retriever puppy. "For you, ma'am."

Puzzled, Stella asked, "But . . . who sent the puppy?"

Turning to leave, he said, "Your husband. Merry Christmas."

She opened the letter from her husband, full of love and

encouragement. He'd purchased the puppy shortly before he died and requested that it be delivered to his wife for Christmas.

As Stella wiped away tears, she picked up the eager puppy, which licked her face while "Joy to the World" played on her radio. Suddenly, she felt incredible delight.[1]

This dying man's thoughtful choice brought present happiness for him, future happiness for her, and happiness to all who hear their story.

Happiness can be natural but not inevitable. It comes naturally when the stage is set for it, by inviting over a good friend, attending an upbeat concert, fixing a nice dinner, joining a small group, or reading the right book. Our actions should be in concert with our prayers—we should pray to find happiness in God and then take the kind of actions that will help us find happiness in him.

Some say, "I thought I would experience joy in the Christian life, but I never have." Is that because we spend hours a day on social media but "don't have time" to join a home Bible study? Do we schedule lunches and tennis matches but not regular times with God? Why do we expect to be happy in God when we're not choosing to do what we can to learn, study, and discuss who God is, what he has done, what he's doing, and what he has promised us?

Research psychologist Martin Seligman says pessimism and depression result from our thought habits. Pessimists believe that bad events will last a long time and will undermine everything they do. Optimists believe that defeat is just a temporary setback and that its causes are confined to this one circumstance. Confronted by a bad situation, optimists perceive it as a challenge, then try harder to deal with it.[2]

Seligman claims that we can change from pessimistic thinking to optimistic thinking. One of the most significant findings in psychology in the past twenty years is that individuals can choose the way they think. This corresponds with Scripture, which tells us we are to "be transformed by the renewing of [our] minds" (Romans 12:2, CEB), and that we should think about things that are good and praiseworthy (see Philippians 4:8).

The Christian life is supernatural but not enchanted. God doesn't magically make us happy despite the fact that we make work, sports, leisure, or sex into our idols. If we choose to seek happiness elsewhere, God won't force himself on us. And he certainly won't give us happiness in what distances us from him.

Happiness comes naturally in the same sense that fruit comes naturally from a tree. If the tree gets sufficient sunshine and water, if the ground is rich in nutrients, if the tree doesn't contract diseases, then yes, it "naturally" produces fruit. We must plant ourselves in the rich soil of God's Word, soak in the living water of God and his people, and bask in the radiant sunlight of his grace. We must take the steps to help and serve others, loving not only God but also our neighbors. Only then, as we change our minds and actions, will newfound happiness come "naturally."

Comparison is deadly. Believing that other people are happier than we are is unproductive and unrealistic. We don't know their struggles, private pains, and secrets. Dennis Prager speaks of those caught in the comparison trap: "They suffer from what can be called compound unhappiness—just as compound interest is interest on interest, compound unhappiness is unhappiness over being unhappy."[3]

If we comparison shop between sin and Jesus, the difference is obvious. One brings you misery; the other, happiness. Why settle for the sin that kills when you can find the happiness in Christ that gives life?

———

Heavenly Father, help us choose to do and to think things that lead to happiness in you. Help us cultivate happiness by making good choices about what goes into our eyes and ears and what comes out of our mouths. Thank you for the example you've set for us and for all the wisdom you've put at our fingertips.

-DAY 46-

What choice do we have when it comes to happiness?

A man without self-control is like a city broken into and left without walls. PROVERBS 25:28

Do not be deceived; happiness and enjoyment do not lie in wicked ways. ISAAC WATTS

OFTEN WE THWART BOTH our own holiness and happiness by going where we don't need to go.

> Do not enter the path of the wicked,
>> and do not walk in the way of the evil.
> Avoid it; do not go on it;
>> turn away from it and pass on.
>
> PROVERBS 4:14-15

This passage has everything to do with happiness. After all, what does sin do? According to Proverbs 1:26-27, it brings calamity, terror, distress, and anguish—in a word, unhappiness. The fruit of sin is self-destruction and fatality (see Proverbs 1:31-33). It brings death and loss (see Proverbs 2:19, 22) as well as great disgrace (see Proverbs 3:35).

I've heard people say, "I don't understand; I prayed for purity, but I fell back into watching Internet pornography. Why didn't God answer my prayer?"

My response? Your choices pulled the rug out from under your prayers. Did you set up a program that restricts your access or informs your friend or pastor when you view pornography? Did you get rid of your computer or move your screen in full view of others? Did you do anything beyond saying a prayer to actually motivate you not to view pornography?

Did you expect God to do everything for you?

I vividly remember a particular counseling appointment as a young pastor, thirty years ago. Eric stormed into my office and flopped into a chair. "I'm really mad at God."

I was startled because Eric was one of the happiest young men I knew. He grew up in a strong churchgoing family, married a sweet Christian woman, and seemed to have a sincere love for Christ.

I asked him why he was mad at God. He explained that for months he'd felt a strong attraction to a woman at his office. She felt the same. "I kept asking God to keep me from immorality, but he let me down."

"Did you ask your wife to pray for you?" I questioned. "Did you stay away from the woman?"

"Well . . . no. We went out for lunch nearly every day."

I looked at Eric and a thought came to me. I started slowly pushing a big book across my desk. As it inched closer to the edge, I prayed aloud, "Lord, please keep this book from falling!"

I kept pushing and praying, while Eric looked at me like I was crazy. Sure enough, as I kept pushing, God didn't suspend the law of gravity, and the book fell to the floor.

"I'm mad at God," I said to Eric. "I asked him to keep my book from falling . . . but he didn't answer my prayer!"[1]

I can still hear the sound of that book hitting the floor. It was a symbol of the trajectory of Eric's life. Instead of calling on God to empower him as he took decisive steps to resist temptation, he kept making unwise choices while asking to be delivered from their natural consequences. Eric went from genuine happiness to misery in a period of just a few years, and eventually he went to jail for sexual crimes. His immorality and sexual abuse didn't come out of the blue. They were the cumulative product of minuscule daily compromises and choices that sabotaged his righteousness and happiness.

Contrast Eric with his friend Rocky. Raised in an unbelieving home, Rocky had sex with a number of women and later came to faith in Christ. Rocky made new choices in keeping with his new nature: immersing himself in the daily meditation of God's Word, joining Bible studies, learning to pray, sharing his faith, and reading great Christian books. He fled from sexual temptations that came his way and guarded his heart and mind. In the process of knowing Christ and following him, Rocky became one of the happiest and most Christ-honoring people I've ever known. To this day, his marriage, family, church involvement, and service to others display the fruit of his wise choices.

Notice how this argument in Proverbs against adultery is an appeal to self-interest:

> Can a man carry fire next to his chest
>> and his clothes not be burned? . . .
> So is he who goes in to his neighbor's wife;
>> none who touches her will go unpunished. . . .
> He who commits adultery lacks sense;
>> he who does it destroys himself.
> He will get wounds and dishonor,
>> and his disgrace will not be wiped away.
>
> PROVERBS 6:27, 29, 32-33

These verses could be summed up this way: making unwise, God-neglecting choices makes us extremely unhappy.

Both Eric and Rocky appeared to have a sincere love for Jesus. Both asked God to help them live righteously. But one failed to cultivate his self-control—he expected God to manage his life and miraculously keep him from the disastrous actions he kept setting himself up to take.

"Make every effort to supplement your . . . knowledge with self-control" (2 Peter 1:5-6). Eric expected God to deliver him from making wrong choices, while Rocky called on God for strength as he did all he could to make right choices.

Both men were defined by their daily choices, which cumulatively produced sin and misery for one and righteousness and happiness for the other.

Holy Spirit, *please give us the wisdom to cry out to you when we're tempted. Help us to flee evil and pursue righteousness. Remind us there will be consequences for our choices and that so much is at stake, including our present and future happiness and the welfare of those we love. Empower us to make wise decisions that honor you instead of expecting you to deliver us from the inevitable consequences of our own actions.*

-DAY 47-

Why should we care about making others happy?

Do nothing from selfishness or empty conceit, but with humility of mind regard one another as more important than yourselves; do not merely look out for your own personal interests, but also for the interests of others.   PHILIPPIANS 2:3-4, NASB

It turns out that choosing to pursue four basic values of faith, family, community and work is the surest path to happiness.
ARTHUR BROOKS

THOUGH I HAVEN'T SEEN them for twenty years, I've never forgotten the father and son who picked up our trash each week. I could hear them singing and laughing. If I was outside when they came by, they'd say, "Have a great day!"—and it was obvious that's what they were having. Likewise, God the Father loves Jesus. It showed in his work, and his Son entered into his Father's happiness.

English architect Sir Christopher Wren (1632–1723) supervised the construction of a number of magnificent cathedrals in London. According to one story, a journalist interviewed some of the workers at a building site. He asked three of them, "What are you doing?"

The first replied, "I'm cutting stone for 10 shillings a day."

The next answered, "I'm putting in 10 hours a day on this job."

The third said, "I'm helping Sir Christopher Wren construct one of London's greatest cathedrals."[1]

Isn't it obvious which of them would be the happiest? There's nothing wrong with working to be paid. But if we see the greater significance of our work—no matter how menial— and we do it all to God's glory, it changes everything.

Psychologist Bernard Rimland conducted a study in which participants were asked to list ten people they knew best and to label them as either happy or not happy. When they finished, they were to go through their lists and this time label each person as selfish or unselfish, using the following definition of selfishness: "A stable tendency to devote one's time and resources to one's own interests and welfare—an unwillingness to inconvenience one's self for others."[2]

What did Rimland discover? According to his research paper "The Altruism Paradox," everyone who was labeled happy was also labeled unselfish. Those "whose activities are devoted to *bringing themselves happiness* . . . are far *less* likely to be happy than those whose efforts are devoted to making others happy." In a remarkable conclusion, he said, "Do unto others as you would have them do unto you."[3]

It's not every day that we see a direct quote from Jesus as the culmination of a psychological study! But the Golden Rule (see Luke 6:31) sums up Rimland's findings perfectly. According to the study, looking out for the interests of others is actually in our own best interest!

Selflessness seems to be strangely counterintuitive to us, perhaps because we imagine that sacrificing for others is an act of holiness that's contrary to happiness. But consider this striking passage, which appeals to us by promising great happiness:

> If you give yourself to the hungry and satisfy the
> desire of the afflicted, then your light will rise in
> darkness and your gloom will become like midday.
> And the LORD will continually guide you, and satisfy
> your desire in scorched places, and give strength to
> your bones; and you will be like a watered garden,
> and like a spring of water whose waters do not fail.
> ISAIAH 58:10-11, NASB

What is gloom but unhappiness? What will satisfy our desires, give us strength, and make us like a watered garden (in short, make us happy)? Giving of ourselves to help others. This is no abstract spiritual blessing—it's a concrete promise of personal happiness!

The "spiritualized" perspective is, "Sacrifice your happiness to devote your life to making others happy." The biblical and true-to-reality perspective is, "Make God, people, and yourself happy at the same time, by serving others."

When we invest ourselves in others, everyone wins.

I enjoy winning. But by God's grace, I've become a gracious loser, which makes me a happier person. When coaching high school tennis, I was playing against our team's number one singles player. We'd played a couple times a week for three years, and he'd never beaten me. But he kept getting better . . . and I didn't. That day, though I tried my best, he beat me for the first time (and by no means the last).

When he won the final point, we both ran to the net and hugged each other, smiling, laughing, and celebrating. I realized, to my surprise, that I was as genuinely happy as he was.

Why was I so happy? Because I had worked hard and long to develop his skills. I had developed vested interests in his victory. His success was my success. And because I loved him, his joy was my joy. "Rejoice with those who rejoice" (Romans 12:15, NIV) had new meaning for me. I realized that when we pour our lives into others, we truly want them to succeed.

Our happiness will always be small as long as we're only happy for ourselves. But when we can be genuinely happy for our spouse, children, grandchildren, neighbors, and friends—and those who live thousands of miles away but benefit from the prayers and money we give to help build wells or translate the Bible into their language—there'll be no end to our happiness.

Arthur Brooks says, "Our brains are actually wired to serve

others. When we give charitable money and service to others, our brain releases several stress hormones which elevate our mood and cause us to feel happy. Serving and giving help to others makes us happier, healthier, more prosperous, and therefore greatly blessed and more successful than non-givers."[4]

Jesus said, "It is more blessed [happy-making] to give than to receive" (Acts 20:35). Yes, we should give because it's right, but also because it's smart. When we give, everyone but Satan wins. God is happy, those who receive our gifts are happy, and we're happy.

God's grace to us is the lightning; our giving to him is the thunder. As lightning precedes thunder, so God's grace precedes and causes our giving. When we give only out of a sense of duty, the joy is far less. When we give because the lightning of God's grace has struck our hearts, then our consequent giving and joy are thunderous.

God, only you could have come up with the idea, arising from your very nature, that giving away ourselves and our things will make us rich beyond belief—rich in relationships and therefore rich in happiness. No one is like you! Thank you for the incredible gift of giving!

-DAY 48-

Can feasts and celebrations please God?

Celebrate the Festival of Shelters for seven days. Also invite the poor, including Levites, foreigners, orphans, and widows. . . . You will be completely happy, so celebrate this festival in honor of the LORD your God. DEUTERONOMY 16:13-15, CEV

As long as that word [holiday] remains, it will always answer the ignorant slander which asserts that religion was opposed to human cheerfulness; that word will always assert that when a day is holy it should also be happy. G. K. CHESTERTON

CECIL RHODES, for whom Rhodesia (now Zimbabwe) was named, was a famous and wealthy businessman, politician, and power broker in South Africa. One evening he sat on a train with Bramwell Booth. Booth could see how depressed Rhodes was and asked him, "Are you a happy man?"

Rhodes responded, "Happy? No!"

Booth then told the influential world figure there was only

one place to find real happiness: "That is at the feet of the crucified Savior, because it is only there we can be freed from our sins." Rhodes responded, pointing toward where Booth's father, General William Booth, founder of the Salvation Army, was sitting: "I would give all I possess to believe what that old man in the next carriage believes!"[1]

He saw in a Christ-follower the happiness he lacked.

Unfortunately, laughter, fun, happiness, and partying are rarely associated with the Bible and Christ-followers today . . . but they should be!

The Bible's many references to singing, dancing, celebrations, feasts, and festivities depict not only worship but delight and pleasure.

Part of what blinds us to God's emphasis on happiness is our knowledge that pagans worshiped pleasure deities and their celebrations centered on drunkenness and immorality. For many of us, celebrating suffers from guilt by association.

The logic goes like this:

- *Since immorality is bad, sex is bad.*
- *Since drunkenness is bad, alcohol is bad.*
- *Since laziness is bad, rest is bad.*
- *Since greed is bad, money is bad.*

We might as well say that since gluttony is bad, food is bad; and since drowning is bad, water is bad. Because sin often happens at parties, some conclude that parties must be sinful. (Of course, sin happens at work and church, too, but people seldom conclude work and church are sinful.)

Proverbs 15:15 says, "The cheerful of heart has a continual feast." A feast is the ultimate picture of happiness—and the Sabbath meant there was at least one feast per week. In addition, there were a number of weeklong festivals that involved eating together daily.

Words describing eating, meals, and food appear more than a thousand times in Scripture, with the English translation "feast" occurring an additional 187 times. Feasting is profoundly relational, marked by conversation, storytelling, and laughter. Biblical feasts were spiritual gatherings that drew attention to God, his greatness, and his redemptive purposes.

Of course, God forbids drunkenness and gluttony (two things that ultimately make us not only unholy but unhappy), but the partying described in Scripture reveals the happiness of the God who invented feasts and festivals, and who commands and encourages singing, dancing, eating, and drinking.

In times of celebration, the people of Israel publicly indulged in the good gifts God had blessed them with. Those gifts included food, wine, music, dance, and fun—all with the understanding that God is the source of everything good and that the enjoyment of his blessings is a happy privilege.

Festivals such as the Feast of Tabernacles included sacrifices for sin (see Leviticus 23:37-41). Sorrow over sin and its redemptive price was real but momentary. Once the sacrifices were complete, the festival became all about being happy in God and one another.

Feasts that recognized repentance, forgiveness, and redemption included more joy than any party pagans could host, because the participants' delight was God centered, deeper, and reality based. "Happy are those whose transgression is forgiven, whose sin is covered!" (Psalm 32:1, NRSV). In light of such good news, who wouldn't want to celebrate?

The church father Chrysostom (347–407) said, "All life is a festival since the Son of God has redeemed you from death."[2]

Historically, God's people always celebrated more than the surrounding nations, never less! Why shouldn't we do the same, since the gospel gives us even more reason to celebrate? Jesus repeatedly mentioned to his disciples that after we're resurrected, we'll eat together, enjoying the company of familiar biblical figures. He said, "Many will come from east and west and recline at table with Abraham, Isaac, and Jacob in the kingdom of heaven" (Matthew 8:11). This must have delighted his listeners.

By building multiple festivities into Israel's calendar, God integrated joy into the lives of his people. These feast days served to link happiness with holiness—two concepts that have become tragically separated from each other in not only the world's thinking but also the church's.

In today's worship settings, "fellowship" has been scaled

back dramatically. It may involve moderate laughter, but rarely does it reflect the great happiness described in the Bible. Indeed, the difference between the grand feast of the Lord's Supper in the New Testament and the symbolic wafers and grape juice offered by most modern churches at Communion is the difference between a great celebration on the one hand and a minimalist ritual on the other.

Spurgeon said this about the most sacred rituals of the church, particularly Communion: "Gospel ordinances are choice enjoyments, enjoined upon us by the loving rule of Him whom we call Master and Lord. We accept them with joy and delight. . . . The Lord's own Supper is a joyful festival, a feast."[3]

Wouldn't it be great if children growing up in Christian homes looked forward to additional God-centered holidays— ones they could invite their unbelieving friends to join? Wouldn't it be fitting if church was known as the place that celebrates more than the world, rather than less? Worship, camaraderie, and unity would be hallmarks of such events. But one of the greatest payoffs would be reestablishing followers of Jesus as people of profound happiness who are quick to celebrate the greatness, goodness, love, grace, and happiness of our God.

God's people ought to say, "Let us eat, drink, and be merry today to celebrate the time when we'll eat, drink, and be merry in a world without suffering and without end!"

Were we to do more of this kind of celebrating, and do it

better, surely fewer of our children, and generations to come, would fall for what may be the enemy's deadliest lie—that the gospel of Jesus doesn't offer happiness and that people must go elsewhere to find it.

———————

Jesus, life with you is a party! We might eagerly go to a party to meet a famous person, but you are the greatest and most famous being in the universe. And you promise you are with us always, and you even live in us! Each meal we eat is an opportunity to dine with you. Life without you would not be worth living. Life with you is worth celebrating now and forever!

-DAY 49-

How can reading God's Word promote lasting happiness?

How sweet Your word is to my taste—sweeter than honey in my mouth. PSALM 119:103, HCSB

The Bible is not an end in itself, but a means to bring men to an intimate and satisfying knowledge of God, that they may enter into Him, that they may delight in His Presence, may taste and know the inner sweetness of the very God Himself in the core and center of their hearts. A. W. TOZER

GEORGE MÜLLER (1805–1898), an Englishman who spent his life caring for thousands of orphans in the 1800s, suffered from bad health and the weight of stressful responsibilities. One day he wrote in his journal, "This morning I greatly dishonored the Lord by irritability manifested toward my dear wife." He said he fell "on my knees before God, praising him for having given me such a wife."[1]

Müller didn't excuse his irritability. He knew his unhappiness and bad mood had displeased God and hurt his wife. He owned up to it. But he couldn't eliminate stress or periodic bad health. So what was his solution? He wrote,

> *I saw more clearly than ever that the first great and primary business to which I ought to attend every day was, to have my soul happy in the Lord. The first thing to be concerned about was, not how much I might serve the Lord, but how I might get my soul into a happy state, and how my inner man might be nourished. . . . I saw that the most important thing I had to do was to give myself to the reading of the Word of God, and to meditation on it.*[2]

On another occasion Müller said, "In what way shall we attain to this settled happiness of soul? How shall we learn to enjoy God? . . . This happiness is to be obtained through the study of the holy Scriptures."[3]

Our happiness is proportionate to our investment in studying God's Word. My conversion to Christ didn't just make me a better person; it made me a happier person. As I've grown closer to Jesus, he has produced in me a deeper and greater happiness. Not because I've seen less evil and suffering—indeed, I've seen far more than I did when I was less happy.

My intellectual life and spiritual life aren't on different tracks. They're inseparable—Jesus said we're to love the Lord our God with our hearts and our minds (see Matthew 22:37).

Had I not taken time to go deep and ponder God and his truth and his ways, all the spiritual inclinations in the world wouldn't have left me with a settled happiness. "As your words came to me I drank them in, and they filled my heart with joy and happiness because I belong to you, O LORD, the God who rules over all" (Jeremiah 15:16, NET).

There's nothing wrong with things such as sports and politics and today's news. But being an expert in those areas doesn't prepare us to live wisely, make Christ-centered decisions, lead our families through hard times, or prepare us to die well. Time in God's Word does.

People are unhappy because they listen to the thousands of unhappy voices clamoring for attention. Joy comes from listening to and believing words of joy from the source of joy. Jesus said, "My sheep hear my voice, and I know them, and they follow me" (John 10:27). When we follow him, we're happy. When we don't, we're not.

Many Christian men would agree that they're experts in business, hunting, fishing, football, or cars. What if they took even half their time devoted to political talk shows and hobbies and invested it in learning solid Bible doctrine through listening to the Bible and reading great Christian books? As many others do, they could converse theologically with as much knowledge and pleasure as they can about sports, hunting, fishing, cars, or politics.

We all talk about what we know best—what's most

important to us. That means we need to change what's important to us by investing more time in it.

How many men have frequent God-centered conversations today—with each other, their wives, and their children? How much pleasure and happiness are we depriving ourselves of by talking about everything except what matters most?

Calvin Miller (1936–2012) lamented, "Never have there been so many disciples who did so little studying. . . . Our day is plagued by hordes of miserable Christians whose pitiful study habits give them few victories and much frustration. Serious students will develop dynamic minds and a confident use of the gifts God has given to them."[4]

Scripture is joy-giving and liberating, not hostile and condemning. On the one hand, the law points out our unrighteousness, leading to our condemnation (see Romans 7:7). On the other hand, the life-giving aspect of the law caused David to happily celebrate it:

- *I delight in your commands because I love them (Psalm 119:47, NIV).*
- *I deeply love your Law! I think about it all day (Psalm 119:97, CEV).*

Spurgeon said, "There is nothing in the Law of God that will rob you of happiness—it only denies you that which would cost you sorrow!"[5]

Only by learning what Scripture says about God can we know what's true about him—and experience the truth-based happiness that flows from him.

———

Holy and awesome God, you alone are worthy of our time and attention. Thank you for the life-giving, happiness-saturated gift of your Word! Help us realize what a treasure it is. May we not settle for anything less than daily seeking you through your Word and enjoying the happiness you've provided for us.

Are health and wealth essential to happiness?

If anyone teaches a different doctrine . . . he is puffed up with conceit . . . imagining that godliness is a means of gain. . . . But those who desire to be rich fall into temptation, into a snare, into many senseless and harmful desires that plunge people into ruin and destruction. For the love of money is a root of all kinds of evils. It is through this craving that some have wandered away from the faith and pierced themselves with many pangs. 1 TIMOTHY 6:3-5, 9-10

He that serves God for money will serve the devil for better wages. SIR ROBERT L'ESTRANGE

PROSPERITY THEOLOGY teaches that God will bless with material abundance and good health those who obey him and lay claim to his promises. "We don't have to wait for God's blessing in the life to come," it promises. "He'll send it to us here and now."

I don't want to be uncharitable, but I will be blunt: I believe prosperity theology, with its practice of twisting some Scriptures while ignoring others, is straight from the pit of Hell. Centered on telling people they deserve whatever they want, this worldview treats God as a genie or a cosmic slot machine: insert a positive confession, pull the lever, catch the winnings.

God's blessing on financial giving is turned into a money-back guarantee of a hundredfold return that will look like whatever we want or claim. Prayer degenerates into coercion by which adherents "name it and claim it," pulling God's leash until he increases their comforts.

It isn't unspiritual to desire health over sickness, wealth over poverty, and success over failure. But if the source of our happiness isn't God, then health, wealth, and success become our false gods. God becomes a mere means to an end.

"Faith" becomes a crowbar to break down the door of God's reluctance rather than a humble attempt to lay hold of his willingness. Sadly, claiming that God must take away an illness or a financial hardship often means calling on him to remove the very things he's permitted and designed to make us more like Christ.

When hard times come, people should lose their faith in false doctrine, not in God. In contrast to jewelry-draped televangelists, Paul said, "We must go through many hardships to enter the kingdom of God" (Acts 14:22, NIV).

When righteous Job lost everything, even his children, he worshiped God, saying, "The LORD gave and the LORD has taken away; may the name of the LORD be praised." We're told, "In all this, Job did not sin by charging God with wrongdoing" (Job 1:21-22, NIV).

In contrast, when advocates of the prosperity gospel lose their health and wealth, they lose their happiness, demonstrating that the true object of their faith wasn't God.

Our prayers are to be earnest, unapologetic requests for what we desire, uttered in willing submission to whatever God wants. True faith doesn't insist that we say, "I'll conquer this cancer." Rather, we can affirm, "I know God can heal me, and I'll ask him to do so. But I trust him. I pray he'll accomplish his best whether through sickness and death or through healing and ongoing life."

Some will write off this kind of prayer as lacking in faith since it acknowledges the possibility of death. But aside from the return of Christ in our lifetimes, which is possible but far from certain, we'll all die. Every single one of us. (Seriously, do you know any 120-year-old faith healers?)

What we need is not faith in faith, but faith in God, the true God of the Bible, who will keep his promise of resurrection and eternal life.

As Easter worked in reverse to make Good Friday good, so our resurrection will work in reverse to bring goodness out of our most difficult days. Faith is a sort of forward memory in which we trust God's promise of eternal happiness and experience a foretaste of that happiness in severe difficulty.

There's an important difference between the health-and-wealth mentality and happiness. The primary source of our happiness isn't our circumstances but our God, who promised he'd be with us always and who commands us to rejoice in him.

By focusing only on resurrection triumph and ignoring God's call and empowerment to take up our crosses and suffer hardship, we're robbed of a biblically grounded and reality-based trust in God, who guarantees that all sorrows will end and that although we have present sorrows, our Savior simultaneously promises us both eternal and present joy.

A life focused on God allows us to rejoice in whatever health and wealth he entrusts to us as stewards but reminds us that he doesn't promise these as permanent conditions in the present world. We're called to give away God's money to help the needy and to fulfill the great commission (see Matthew 6:19-21; see also 1 Timothy 6:6-10, 17-19).

Some Christians are also called upon to sacrifice their health through long hours of labor or by enduring persecution. We should be willing to lay everything on the line for Jesus because our life focus is on God, not self, health, or wealth—and not happiness either, in any form other than happiness in God, which is his command and calling. It's not that material things are inherently bad; they just can't keep their promise of happiness. Only God can.

If our happiness is grounded in God, we won't lose the

basis for it, because nothing will separate us from the love of Christ (see Romans 8:37-39).

An Iranian Christ-follower spoke at our church. His dear friend in prison, who'd been separated from his family for three years, writes, "They say I'm the happiest man in this prison, and I believe they're right."

The gladness of God's children isn't the pasted-on, fake-it-till-you-make-it "joy" of the health-and-wealth gospel, but the deep and resonant happiness of someone who knows that the God with the nail-scarred hands loves him and is truly with him even in prison.

Lord, please forgive us for treating you like a vending machine or a genie, thinking we can get whatever we want whenever we want it without regard to your glory and sovereign plan. Teach us that we'll never be truly, deeply, and lastingly happy until we recognize that you give us everything we need because you are everything we need . . . and nothing will ever separate us from your love.

-DAY 51-

How does forgiveness relate to our happiness?

O the happiness of him whose transgression [is] forgiven, whose sin is covered.   PSALM 32:1, YLT

Christians are happy, real ones, because they know that their sins are all forgiven.   R. A. TORREY

RUTH BELL GRAHAM told the story of Alexander Grigolia, a brilliant but unhappy immigrant to the United States from Soviet Georgia. He was struck by the demeanor of the man who shined his shoes. One day, looking down at this man who worked cheerfully and enthusiastically, and considering his own misery, Grigolia asked, "Why are you always so happy?"

Surprised, the man said, "Jesus. He loves me. He died so God could forgive my badness. He makes me happy."

Grigolia said nothing in response but could not escape those simple words. Eventually he came to faith in Christ, became a college professor, and had a strong influence on his students, one being future evangelist Billy Graham.[1]

Anyone unaware of his or her guilt before a holy God is in the worst possible condition. What if a person with a burst appendix couldn't feel pain? He might happily stay home and watch a movie rather than go to the hospital. And then he would die.

Satan is the enemy of God's happiness and ours. While he can't rob God of happiness, he specializes in sabotaging ours, catching us on the baited hook of pleasure. The first hit of a drug, the buzz of alcohol, or the thrill of illicit sex seems so good at the time. But then the very thing that brings us a taste of joy robs us of true and abiding joy. Sin is the ultimate killjoy.

To sin is to break relationship with God. Therefore, sin is the biggest enemy of happiness and forgiveness its greatest friend. Confession reunites us with the God of happiness.

If we truly believe that sin is never in our best interests, it will clarify many otherwise hard decisions in which we imagine we must choose between helping people do right and helping them be happy.

For instance, a young woman who believed that abortion takes the life of an innocent child nonetheless told me that because she loved her friend, she was going to drive her to the clinic to get an abortion. She said, "That's what you do when you love someone, even if you disagree."

I asked, "If your friend decided to kill her mother and had a shotgun in hand, would you drive her to her mother's house?"

"Of course not!"

But other than legality, what's the difference? Too often, in the name of love, we assist people in taking wrong actions which, because they're wrong, will rob them of happiness. We may congratulate ourselves for being "loving," but what good does our love do if it encourages their self-destruction? It's only when she and her friend acknowledge their individual sin and seek God's forgiveness that they can be restored to the happiness a kind and gracious God has waiting for them.

We fall for Satan's lies over and over again. But God tells us the truth about what will make us happy. Our ultimate happiness hinges on whom we choose to believe.

Jesus said, "If your right eye makes you stumble, tear it out and throw it from you; for it is better for you to lose one of the parts of your body, than for your whole body to be thrown into hell" (Matthew 5:29, NASB). In moments of strength, we need to make godly decisions in preparation for moments of weakness. For example, we shouldn't put ourselves in places and with people or objects that move us toward sin (including anything with Internet access if pornography or social media is a problem).

I received an e-mail from a young man at college who gave up his virginity. His utter despair was palpable. Of course, an unbeliever might think his misery was due to "unnecessary" guilt feelings. But in this case, they were accurate indicators of genuine guilt.

This young man might feel temporarily happier if he

denied his guilt, just as someone jumping from a plane, not realizing his parachute is defective, can be temporarily exhilarated as he falls. But the moment he understands his true condition, he'll be terrified. If he has a backup parachute, the man's realization will serve him well. Likewise, if this young man repents and embraces Christ's forgiveness, the crushing feelings of guilt that brought him to repentance will be God's grace to him—his backup parachute.

David chose the sin of adultery and subsequent murder to cover up his sin so he could be happy. Yet his groaning caused his body to waste away.

But his confession changed everything:

> Then I acknowledged my sin to you,
>   and I did not hide my iniquity;
> I said, "I will confess my transgressions to the LORD,"
>   and you forgave the guilt of my sin.
>
> PSALM 32:5, NRSV

David went on to describe the relationship with the one who delivered him from the unhappiness of sin:

> You are a hiding place for me;
>   you preserve me from trouble;
>   you surround me with glad cries of deliverance.
>
> PSALM 32:7

Spurgeon said, "It does not spoil your happiness . . . to confess your sin. The unhappiness is in not making the confession."[2]

Martin Luther said, "Sin is pure unhappiness, forgiveness pure happiness."[3] It's hard to imagine a more concise and accurate statement. Sin must be dealt with directly through awareness, confession, and repentance. Only in forgiveness can we have relational oneness with God and, hence, enduring happiness. If we believe this biblically grounded truth, our lives will be transformed.

Jesus, thank you for all you've done to make it possible for us to live in eternal happiness with you. Help us to see sin for what it truly is. Allow us to embrace your forgiveness and then freely extend it to others. For your sake and ours, please make us sorry for our sin so we will turn to you, confess earnestly, and experience the freedom and happiness of forgiveness. You made such a horrific sacrifice because of our sin, and we're forever grateful for your incredible eagerness to forgive us. Saying thank you is not enough, but we say it anyway, from the depths of our souls.

Must we choose between holiness and happiness?

Happy and holy is the one who shares in the first resurrection!
REVELATION 20:6, PHILLIPS

This first act of divine sovereign pleasure concerning us, was the choosing of us from all eternity unto holiness and happiness. JOHN OWEN

AS A YOUNG PASTOR, I preached, as others still do, "God calls us to holiness, not happiness."[1] This sounds spiritual, and there's a half-truth to it. I saw Christians pursue what they thought would make them happy, falling headlong into sexual immorality, alcoholism, materialism, and obsession with success. They'd turned from holiness, and the lure of happiness appeared to me to be at odds with holiness.

I was attempting to oppose our human tendency to put preferences and convenience before obedience to Christ. It sounded God honoring to say, "God wants you holy, not happy," and I could quote countless authors and preachers who had persuaded me of this (though I confess I hadn't carefully thought it through).

There were several flaws in my thinking, including inconsistency with my own experience. I'd found profound happiness in Christ; wasn't that from God? Furthermore, calling people to reject happiness in favor of holiness was ineffective. It might work for a while but not in the long run, given the reality that all people inherently seek happiness.

It has become common for Christians to draw a line between the holiness we know we should seek and the happiness we do seek. We see the world seeking happiness instead of holiness. Therefore, we assume we should do the opposite. But we're wrong.

Tony Reinke gets it right: "Sin is joy poisoned. Holiness is joy postponed and pursued."[2] Christians fear happiness because they think it entails irresponsibility and negligence. Some Christians see happiness as the opposite of holiness. But Scripture says otherwise.

Consider Leviticus 9:24: "Fire came out from the presence of the LORD and consumed the burnt offering . . . on the altar. And when all the people saw it, they shouted for joy and fell facedown" (NIV). The radically holy God sent down fire, and they did what? They fell facedown . . . and "shouted for joy"!

This remarkable response flows from the utter holiness of submission combined with the utter happiness of praise. To fall facedown before the infinitely holy God while shouting for joy is a stunning picture of redemptive glory!

In his exegetical treatment of the Psalms, Mark Futato affirms that happiness and holiness are the book's two dominant themes. He argues, "A holy life, according to the book of Psalms, results in a happy life . . . a life lived in keeping with God's instructions."[3]

Any understanding of God that's incompatible with the lofty and infinitely holy view of God in Ezekiel 1:26-28 and Isaiah 6:1-4, along with the powerful view of the glorified Christ in Revelation 1, is utterly false. God is decidedly and unapologetically anti-sin, but in no sense anti-happiness. Indeed, holiness is what secures our happiness.

Too often our message to the world becomes a false gospel that lays upon people an impossible burden. "Give up happiness; choose holiness instead" is not good news in any sense, and therefore it is not the true gospel! It bears more resemblance to the legalistic worldview of the Pharisees Jesus condemned (see Matthew 23:2-4).

If we believe the lie that saying no to sin means saying no to happiness, then no amount of self-restraint will keep us from ultimately seeking happiness in sin.

The wonderful news is that holiness doesn't mean abstaining from pleasure; holiness means recognizing Jesus as the source of life's greatest pleasure.

If given a choice, people who grow up in evangelical

churches will predictably choose what appears to be the delightful happiness of the world over the dutiful holiness of the church. Satan tries to rig the game by leading us to believe we can't have both happiness and holiness. Offer people a choice between being hungry and thirsty or having food and drink, and their choice is obvious. Never mind that the meal may be laced with cyanide or the drink injected with arsenic. Any offer of happiness, with or without holiness, will always win over an offer of holiness devoid of happiness.

DNA's double helix is perfectly balanced at the core of human life. Two strands wrap around each other, forming an axis of symmetry and providing a perfect complement for each other.

God has made holiness and happiness to enjoy a similar relationship: each benefits from the other. For those of us who are Christ-centered believers, our lives should overflow with both. Neither alone will suffice; both together are essential for the truly Christ-centered life.

When Jesus says, "Be perfect" (Matthew 5:48), we should recognize that true happiness in him is part of what he intends. Our pleasure is won in the "Aha!" moments of discovering firsthand why God's ways really are best. As we grow in knowledge, we can increasingly join Paul in saying, "We have the mind of Christ" (1 Corinthians 2:16) on the things he has revealed. The more we discover God's ways and experience the goodness of his holiness, the less we try to find happiness apart from him.

Must we choose between holiness and happiness?

Holy and happy Father, loving you is our only true path to happiness. You've said that when we delight in you, your desires become ours. Thank you for making the life of true holiness a glad life with abundant delights!

-DAY 53-

Is seeking happiness selfish?

I will sacrifice with shouts of joy; I will sing and make music to the LORD. PSALM 27:6, NIV

Nothing that you have not given away will ever be really yours. Nothing in you that has not died will ever be raised from the dead. Look for yourself, and you will find in the long run only hatred, loneliness, despair, rage, ruin, and decay. But look for Christ and you will find Him, and with Him everything else thrown in. C. S. LEWIS

MANY CHRISTIANS BELIEVE the notion that wanting to be happy is inherently selfish and immoral. Why? Partly because we focus on one group of biblical statements without balancing them with others. True, the Bible warns against those who are "lovers of self," identifying them as money-loving, boastful, proud, abusive, and unholy (see 2 Timothy 3:2). The self-love spoken of here is obviously wrong. But when Jesus tells us to love our neighbors as ourselves (see Matthew 22:39), he isn't arguing that we shouldn't love ourselves, only that we should extend our instincts for self-care to caring for others.

Flight crews routinely announce, "If you're traveling with a child or someone who requires assistance, in the case of an emergency, secure your own oxygen mask first before helping the other person." Those instructions may sound selfish, just as it sounds selfish to say that one of our main duties in life is to find happiness in God. But only when we're delighting in our Lord do we have the happiness of God to offer everyone else. If we don't take the time and effort to cultivate that happiness, we can't help those around us.

It's possible for someone to act sacrificially and selflessly in the best interests of others while enjoying the fruit, including feeling good about having honored God and receiving his approval and reward.

The pediatric surgeon who serves in remote African villages for minimal pay is by some standards making a huge sacrifice. After all, she could make ten times the money in an American hospital: better hours, higher success rates, and lavish living.

However, while she sacrifices conveniences to serve others, she is not sacrificing happiness. She's happiest while using her gifts and skills to help people, knowing that by God's grace she's saving lives and improving children's quality of life. She enjoys the teary gratitude of parents who thought their child's cleft palate or inability to walk could never be corrected.

So she sacrifices something small to gain something great.

Those self-sacrificing yet self-gratifying physicians are living examples of what Jesus says: "If anyone would come after me, let him deny himself and take up his cross daily and follow me. For whoever would save his life will lose it, but whoever loses his life for my sake will save it. For what does it profit a man if he gains the whole world and loses or forfeits himself?" (Luke 9:23-25). Similarly, Matthew records Jesus as saying, "Whoever finds his life will lose it, and whoever loses his life for my sake will find it" (Matthew 10:39).

Many think that Jesus' primary message here is the virtue of selflessness and self-sacrifice. But take another look: he calls us to lose our lives for his sake by appealing to our desire to find our lives and save them! By honoring and following Christ, we do the best possible thing for ourselves!

C. S. Lewis began his great sermon "The Weight of Glory,"

If you asked twenty good men today what they thought the highest of the virtues, nineteen of them would reply, Unselfishness. But if you had asked almost any of the great Christians of old, he would have replied, Love. You see what has happened? A negative term has been substituted for a positive. . . . The negative idea of Unselfishness carries with it the suggestion not primarily of securing good things for others, but of going without them ourselves, as if our abstinence and not their happiness was the important point.[1]

Lewis went on to make this critical point: "The New Testament has lots to say about self-denial, but not about self-denial as an end in itself. We are told to deny ourselves and to take up our crosses in order that we may follow Christ; and nearly every description of what we shall ultimately find if we do so contains an appeal to desire."[2]

We are quick to recognize that Satan tempts us through offers of happiness and gain. However, we're slower to recognize how he tempts us by offering a twist on our God-given desires.

If God has wired us to want happiness, surely we shouldn't imagine it is wrong to want happiness. We just need to listen to God, not Satan, about where to find it. A high salary and good benefits will motivate someone to accept a position only if that person values big paychecks and perks. The draw of an academic credential, a sales award, an Olympic medal, or a Super Bowl ring all hinge upon one's desire for such things.

I've had countless conversations with sincere Christians who imagine it's selfish and wrong to desire the rewards God himself offers them. Yet Jesus repeatedly offered his followers rewards as motivations to follow him (see Matthew 6:6, 17-18; 25:37-40; Luke 6:22-23, 35, 38; 14:12-14). Since Christ appeals to our yearning for reward, which is a matter of personal gain, wanting reward and gain cannot be intrinsically wrong—God would never appeal to our desire for what's sinful, because he never tempts us (see James 1:13).

Therefore we should want whatever Jesus offers us.

Jesus said, "The kingdom of heaven is like treasure hidden in a field. When a man found it, he hid it again, and then in his joy went and sold all he had and bought that field" (Matthew 13:44, NIV). Should we feel sorry for this man? After all, he "sold all he had"—the poor man! But Jesus said he did this "in his joy." He surrendered a lesser treasure to obtain a far greater one. The cost/benefit ratio was totally in his favor! We should seize our opportunity to part with small temporary treasures to gain great everlasting treasures (see Matthew 6:19-21).

When God calls upon us to deny ourselves and follow him, what appears to be our loss is in fact our gain. Should we want to gain our lives? Of course. Paradoxically and beautifully, losing our lives to Christ is the *means* to ultimately finding them.

Lord, your ways are so different from ours. Your ways bring happiness when ours bring only misery, frustration, broken relationships, and hopelessness. Remove our false guilt for wanting to experience fulfillment and gladness. Enable us to find ourselves and our happiness by losing ourselves in you.

-DAY 54-

Can self-forgetfulness make us happier?

Let each of you look not only to his own interests, but also to the interests of others. Have this mind among yourselves, which is yours in Christ Jesus, who, though he was in the form of God, did not count equality with God a thing to be grasped, but emptied himself, by taking the form of a servant, being born in the likeness of men. PHILIPPIANS 2:4-7

The thing we would remember from meeting a truly gospel-humble person is how much they seemed to be totally interested in us. Because the essence of gospel-humility is not thinking more of myself or thinking less of myself, it is thinking of myself less. TIMOTHY KELLER

ON THE FIRST DAY OF a long-awaited two-week vacation, I found out that a book I'd labored on intensely had been altered for the worse, and I had no recourse. It was the one and only time in thirty years of writing that the published book would be inferior to the manuscript I'd submitted. It was the

low point in my professional life. I was disappointed not only by what had happened but also by how deeply it affected me. If you've ever been disappointed by your own disappointment, you understand. ("I should be bigger than this—how come I'm not?")

We were at our friends' house on Maui. Despite the beautiful surroundings, I stewed over this writing project, even though I realized I'd eventually gain perspective. (I did, but not until after the vacation; I just wanted to fast-forward to when I knew I'd feel better!) Meanwhile, I snorkeled for three hours a day. That was the only time when the cloud dramatically lifted. Floating and diving among the beautiful fish, turtles, eels, and sharks—and enjoying a magical hour and a half swimming with that monk seal I named Molly—I lost myself in these creatures and the God who made them. I forgot about myself, my shortcomings, others' failings, and my disappointments.

I left my troubled self on the shore. As long as my face was underwater, I was free and happy. It was only when I got out of the water and came back to "Randy's world" that my happiness vaporized.

Sometimes when times are tough, I have that same experience of losing myself during quiet times with God. Sometimes I have it when laughing with family and friends. Other times it's when I'm riding a bike or listening to music or a great audiobook. C. S. Lewis said of the humble person, "He will not be thinking about humility: he will not be thinking about himself at all."[1] I've seen the truth of what Lewis and Tim Keller and others have discovered, experiencing my greatest happiness not simply when I think less of myself, but when I think of myself less. When I'm thinking most about Jesus and others, and least about me, I'm most fulfilled.

These lines from a novel ring true:

> *When you're unhappy, you get to pay a lot of attention to yourself. And you get to take yourself oh so very seriously. Your truly happy people . . . don't think about themselves very much. Your unhappy person resents it when you try to cheer him up, because that means he has to stop dwellin' on himself and start payin' attention to the universe. Unhappiness is the ultimate form o' self-indulgence.*[2]

People who think a lot about themselves and their plans for wealth and success—e.g., writing a bestselling book and being mentioned in the same sentence with Hemingway—tend to be unhappy.

However, people who think a lot about Christ and his grace, the great doctrines of the faith, and how to love and serve others tend to be happy people. By redirecting attention from ourselves to God, we adopt a right perspective that brings happiness. Just as I revise my writing to make it better, I must revise my beliefs and thought habits in light of God's Word. Happiness isn't my exclusive goal, of course, but it's certainly a welcome by-product.

Psalm 37:4 reads, "Delight yourself in the LORD." Not "sit there and wait for the Lord to delight you." It's active, not passive. We aren't spoon-fed his pleasures; we need to go to the banquet, reach out our hands, and eat that delicious cuisine. As surely as it's our responsibility to put good food in our mouths, it's our responsibility to move our thoughts toward God and be happy in him!

We need to stop consuming our self-preoccupied thoughts and instead cultivate our appetite for God and what's true about him: "Taste and see that the LORD is good. How happy is the man who takes refuge in Him!" (Psalm 34:8, HCSB).

When I contemplate Christ—when I meditate on his unfathomable love and grace—I lose myself in him. When he's the center of my thinking, before I know it, I'm happy.

Tim Keller writes,

> *Don't you want to be the kind of person who, when they see themselves in a mirror or reflected in a shop window, does not admire what they see but does not cringe either? . . . Wouldn't you like to be the skater who wins the silver, and yet is thrilled about those three triple jumps that the gold medal winner did? To love it the way you love a sunrise? Just to love the fact that it*

*was done? You are as happy that they did it as if you
had done it yourself. . . . This is gospel-humility, blessed
self-forgetfulness.*[3]

As commendable as such humility is, we can never achieve
it simply by willing it to appear. Otherwise, we'll be thinking
about ourselves and our valiant attempts to be humble. What
we need is to be so gripped by Jesus and his grace, so lost in
his love, that we truly forget about ourselves. Why would we
want to think about ourselves, the lesser, when we can think
about him, the infinitely greater? This happens directly, when
we worship and serve him, and also indirectly, when we love
and serve others for his glory.

*Lord Jesus, this side of Heaven we'll never completely
forget about ourselves, but by your grace, help us more
and more to turn our focus away from ourselves and
toward you so we can experience the happiness of self-
forgetfulness. Show us how we can better serve others, not
just ourselves. Thank you for motivating and helping us to
help others—for your gladness, as well as theirs and ours.*

What does thankfulness have to do with happiness?

Let them sacrifice thank offerings and tell of his works with songs of joy.   PSALM 107:22, NIV

When someone continually talks about how happy they are, I tend to doubt them; but when they talk about how grateful they are, I know they have found happiness.   ROB HAWKINS

I HEARD A STORY OF someone who asked a man why he was so happy. The man picked up a binder filled with hundreds of handwritten pages and explained, "Every time someone does something kind for me, I write it in this book. And every time I feel very good about something, I write it in this book."

The questioner said, "I wish I could be as happy as you."

"If you kept a book like this, you would be."

"But the book is so big . . . I haven't had many kind things done for me, and I haven't felt good very often."

"I might have thought that too, if I hadn't recorded them

all. I've learned to see and remember and be grateful for kindness and happiness when they come. Try it. Every time you doubt, read your entries and you'll see all you have to be grateful for."

There are always reasons to be thankful. Matthew Henry, the Puritan preacher and Bible commentator, made this statement after a thief stole his money: "Let me be thankful first because I was never robbed before; second, although they took my purse, they did not take my life; third, because, although they took my all, it was not much; and fourth, because it was I who was robbed, not I who robbed."[1]

Before church, I sometimes speak with a man who has faced difficult life circumstances: his son died, he's battled cancer, he lost his job, and he's feeling the pains of old age. But the smile on his face is genuine. He speaks of the goodness of God and how grateful he is for Jesus, his Savior. He's a truly happy man. I enter the church service feeling I've already met with the Lord and heard a great message, all from my encounter with this brother.

One weekend I walked through our church parking lot and asked another man how he was doing. He launched into a litany of complaints that continued through the hallways and foyer as we headed to worship. He was profoundly unhappy.

He answered my question honestly. But just because a perspective is transparently shared doesn't mean it isn't in dire need of adjustment.

These two men taught me a lesson I've seen thousands of times: with gratitude there's happiness; without it, there's unhappiness. Every time.

In the story of the Prodigal Son in Luke 15, when the younger brother returns home to much rejoicing, the older brother questions his father's actions. The older brother is full of complaints, revealing his proud, ungrateful heart. In the same way, whenever we believe that our heavenly Father is mismanaging our lives and treating others better, we're demonstrating arrogance and ungratefulness. The older brother was as unhappy in his self-righteousness as the younger brother had been in his immorality. But because the prodigal repented and welcomed his father's grace, he was now forgiven, restored, and happy. Yet the older brother, offended by grace and poisoned by ingratitude, remained unhappy.

While researching my novel *Dominion* in 1995, I spent time in Jackson, Mississippi, with legendary pastor, author, and civil rights activist John Perkins. At the age of sixteen, John's brother was shot on the streets by a deputy sheriff and died in John's arms. Twenty years later, John was tortured in a Mississippi jail cell while his wife and children stood outside hearing his cries. But John's heart is full of grace and forgiveness, and he's been a pioneer in racial reconciliation.

John walked me through the streets of Jackson, telling me

story after story, giving credit to Jesus. He took me into a thrift store, where he found an old hat on sale for twenty-five cents. He tried it on for me, flashed his big smile, and asked how it looked. I told him it looked snazzy. John just couldn't get over finding this hat—and at such a great price. I'll never forget his sheer delight at this treasure he'd discovered. It seemed not to occur to him that this very thrift store was under the umbrella of one of the ministries he'd launched.

John and I waited in line, and once at the counter, John handed the girl a quarter, beaming at his find. Recognizing the founder of the ministry, she was surprised and said, "Dr. Perkins, there's no charge for you!"

But John refused to accept special treatment. He insisted she take the quarter and proudly put on his hat. You'd have thought he'd found a priceless treasure!

Every time I looked at John Perkins throughout the day, it made me smile. Even now, decades later, I'm smiling. It was such a little thing, yet it brought such happiness for a man who, in all the sorrows of life and in the greatness of his cause, has never diminished his God-centered appreciation for life's smallest joys.

Good days pleasantly surprise the humble. Even on a difficult day, their hearts overflow with gratitude. They're happy because while most people think they deserve better than what they receive, the grateful truly believe that by God's grace they've received better than they deserve.

———

God, eternity won't be long enough to thank you for all you've given us and all you will give us in the ages to come. May we not wait until we see you for our every breath to be filled with gratitude for the saving work of Jesus . . . along with every secondary gift you give us. May our hearts overflow with gratitude to you each day!

-DAY 56-

Do we have a right to expect happiness in a world of worry?

Happy are you when people hate you, reject you, insult you,
and say that you are evil, all because of the Son of Man!
Be glad when that happens and dance for joy, because
a great reward is kept for you in heaven.
JESUS (LUKE 6:22-23, GNT)

Live, then, and be happy, beloved children of my heart! and
never forget, that until the day God will deign to reveal the
future to man, all human wisdom is contained in these two
words—"Wait and Hope." ALEXANDRE DUMAS

THERE'S A STORY OF a man and his granddaughter who are sitting on a park bench when a traveler asks, "Is this a friendly town? I come from a town full of conflict. Is that what I'll find here?"

The grandfather replies, "Yes, my friend, I'm certain that's what you'll find." Saddened, the traveler continues on.

Before long, another traveler stops. "I come from a village with many delightful people. I wonder, would I find such charming people here?"

The grandfather smiles in response. "Welcome, friend! Yes, you certainly will!"

As the stranger walks away, the puzzled child asks, "Grandfather, why did you give those strangers two different answers to the same question?"

The grandfather answered, "The first man was looking for conflict, while the second was looking for goodness. Each will find exactly what he expects."

We bring ourselves to every situation, every encounter, every relationship. The unhappy person who leaves North Dakota in search of happiness in California finds more sunshine and less snow, but not more happiness. The happy Californian who relocates finds that his happiness accompanies him.

Disneyland claims to be the happiest place on Earth, but according to *60 Minutes*, studies show the happiest nation on Earth is Denmark. What's their secret? Low expectations. Danes have more modest dreams than Americans, and they're less distressed when their hopes don't materialize.[1]

The general view of life in Denmark is somewhat compatible with the doctrine of the Fall: instead of being surprised when life doesn't go their way, Danes are grateful that things aren't worse, and they're happily surprised by health and success. If they have food, clothing, shelter, friends, and family, life seems good.

There's a biblical basis for both realistic and positive expectations. We certainly live in a world with suffering and death. But as believers, we understand that God is with us and won't forsake us and that one day we'll live on a redeemed Earth far happier than Denmark or Disneyland on their best days!

Worry is the product of high stakes and low control. There's no greater enemy of happiness. Worry says that if we care, we should worry—as if that will help somehow. In fact, worry has absolutely no redemptive value. Jesus asked, "Who of you by worrying can add a single hour to your life?" (Luke 12:25, NIV). Nothing is more impotent than worry, and nothing so robs us of happiness in Christ.

Just after instructing us to rejoice in the Lord, Paul writes in Philippians 4:6, "Do not be anxious about anything." Worry is a killjoy. It specializes in worst-case scenarios. In contrast, God tells his children there is much that should make us rejoice:

- *He has already rescued us from the worst, which is eternal Hell.*
- *Even if something terrible happens, he uses it for our eternal good.*
- *Often bad things don't happen, and our worry proves groundless.*

- *Whether or not bad things happen, our worry helps nothing and hurts much.*
- *The cause for all our worries—sin and the Curse— is temporary and will soon be behind us. Forever.*

The command to rejoice is not mere pretense, unrealistic expectations, or positive thinking. Rather, it's embracing our present life, which includes suffering. But even before God wipes it all away, he gives us compelling reasons to rejoice.

Jesus emphatically commands us not to worry (see Matthew 6:25, 34). But how can we avoid worry? A big part of it is adjusting our expectations based on his promises not only that all will be well one day in Heaven but that he is at work here and now, lovingly accomplishing his purposes in our lives.

Max Lucado tells of a boy on the beach who eagerly scoops up and packs sand, creating a magnificent castle. All afternoon he builds a tower, walls, and even a moat. Not far away, a man in his office shuffles papers into stacks and delegates assignments. He punches buttons on a phone and keys on a keyboard, makes profits, and builds his own castle.

In both cases, time passes, the tide rises, and the castles are destroyed. But there's a big difference. The boy expects what's coming and celebrates it. He smiles as his castle erodes and turns into no more than formless lumps in the sand.

Unlike the boy, the businessman is unprepared for what will happen. As life ebbs and flows, the works of his hands are swept away. If his castle isn't taken from him, he'll be taken from his castle. But he chooses not to think about this. While the boy has no sorrow and regret, the man does all he can to hold on to his castle and is inconsolable when his life or house or business slips away.[2]

No matter what comes today or tomorrow, may these words from the Lord to his people Israel become our expectation of the life God ultimately intends for all his children: "I know the plans I have in mind for you, declares the LORD; they are plans for peace, not disaster, to give you a future filled with hope" (Jeremiah 29:11, CEB).

———————

Father of all happiness, we expect things to go our way and are quickly disappointed when they don't. We look so many places other than you for our contentment. Help us to lower our expectations of a stress-free life while raising our expectations of who you are and the happiness you have for us—not only forever, but now. Deliver us from joy-killing worry, and empower us to ground our optimism on the breathtaking eternal realities you've promised us in Christ!

-DAY 57-

What does God promise us about eternal happiness?

Multitudes who sleep in the dust of the earth will awake: some to everlasting life, others to shame and everlasting contempt. Those who are wise will shine like the brightness of the heavens, and those who lead many to righteousness, like the stars for ever and ever. DANIEL 12:2-3, NIV

Christian, meditate much on heaven, it will help thee to press on, and to forget the toil of the way. This vale of tears is but the pathway to the better country: this world of woe is but the stepping-stone to a world of bliss. . . . And, after death, what cometh? What wonder-world will open upon our astonished sight? CHARLES SPURGEON

IN AD 60, SENECA, the Roman Stoic philosopher and states-man who advised Nero, wrote, "No happiness lasts for long."[1] At that same time, the apostle Paul and others were spreading the good news that happiness is in God and will last forever. About five years later, Seneca died in Rome and Paul shortly after, both by Nero's decree. Three years later, when the political tide turned against him, Nero killed himself.

Happiness is short lived . . . unless death is not the end of us and the world, and a happy life in a happy world awaits us still. For people with no faith in God, who deny the Resurrection, these are the best days, and certainly they're winding down to a fixed end. But for genuine Christ-followers, these are decidedly not the best days of our lives. In fact, the best by far is yet to come!

A. W. Tozer said, "When the followers of Jesus Christ lose their interest in heaven they will no longer be happy Christians, and when they are no longer happy Christians they cannot be a powerful force in a sad and sinful world. It may be said with certainty that Christians who have lost their enthusiasm about the Savior's promises of heaven-to-come have also stopped being effective in Christian life and witness in this world."[2]

A culturally engaged young man who's a bestselling author with a large following interviewed me concerning my book *Heaven*. Before the interview, he told me apologetically, "Truth is, I didn't read your book."

I had read his books, so I smiled and said, "Let me guess why. It's because you think Heaven will be boring, and it's the beauties and wonders of this life—the natural world and human culture and the arts—that you're really interested in."

Surprised, he said, "Yes!"

"That's exactly why you should read it," I said. "It's about the New Earth the Bible reveals, a place with resurrected people on a resurrected planet; with resurrected nature, nations, and cultures; with animals, art, music, literature, drama, and galaxies—all for the glory of God."

His eyes brightened and then faded, as if to say, "If only that were true."

Well, it is true. The gospel—the Good News—is way better than we believe it to be. But if we pay attention when we read the Bible, we'll see it:

> Be happy and rejoice forevermore over what I
> am about to create! For look, I am ready to create
> Jerusalem to be a source of joy, and her people to be
> a source of happiness. Jerusalem will bring me joy,
> and my people will bring me happiness. The sound
> of weeping or cries of sorrow will never be heard in
> her again.
>
> ISAIAH 65:18-19, NET

Most of us don't live as if we believe in God's promise of a New Earth. When we hang on, white-knuckled, to this life, it proves our disbelief in an afterlife that is physical (with real health), material (with real wealth), social (with real culture and relationships), and personal (with real happiness and continuance of our identity).

Despite Scripture's claim to the contrary, even Christians

notes

DAY 11: *What's the Difference between Joy and Happiness?*

1. George Vaillant, "The Difference Joy Makes: Finding Contentment through Psychotherapy and Christian Faith," Conference at the Institute of Religion, Houston, October 8–9, 1998.
2. Joni Eareckson Tada, *Joni and Friends Daily Devotional*, November 28, 2013.
3. Charles H. Spurgeon, "God Rejoicing in the New Creation" (Sermon #2211).

DAY 12: *If Happiness Isn't Joy, What Is?*

1. George E. Vaillant, *Spiritual Evolution: A Scientific Defense of Faith* (New York: Broadway Books, 2008), 124.
2. Dawn Wyant, "One Word 2013," *Thoughts and Ponderings* (blog), January 7, 2013, http://morningstardawn.blogspot.com/2013/01/one-word-2013.html.
3. Ibid.
4. C. Hollis Crossman, "The Opposite of Happiness," *The 300 (Judges 7): Lay Theology for the Faithful* (blog), August 7, 2012, http://cholliscrossman.blogspot.com/2012/08 /the-opposite-of-happiness.html.
5. Jackie Lopina, "Loving Your Friend through Infertility: What to Pray For," *Hoping in God* (blog), May 2, 2011, http://jackielopina.wordpress.com/2011/05/02/loving -your-friend-through-infertility-what-to-pray-for-part-3/.
6. Amy H., "Happiness Is Not Joy: Joy Is Better," *The Rusk and Bannock Project* (blog), March 4, 2015, http://ruskandbannock.com/2015/03/04/happiness-is-not-joy-joy -is-better/.
7. Steve Austin, "Happiness Is the Enemy of Joy," *Grace Is Messy* (blog), January 29, 2016, http://www.patheos.com/blogs/graceismessy/2016/01/29/happiness-is-the -enemy-of-joy/.
8. Amy Pardue, "What's Wrong with Pursuing Happiness?" *Hunger for Him* (blog), February 25, 2010, http://hungerforhim.blogspot.com/2010/02/whats-wrong-with -pursuing-happiness.html.

DAY 13: *Is Happiness the World's Imitation of Joy?*

1. Oswald Chambers, *My Utmost for His Highest* (Grand Rapids, MI: Discovery House, 2006), 31.
2. Dorcas Willis, *The Journey Called Ministry* (Bloomington, IN: AuthorHouse, 2013), 41.
3. Celeste P. Walker, *Joy: The Secret of Being Content* (Hagerstown, MD: Review and Herald, 2005), 65.
4. S. D. Gordon, quoted in Billy Graham, *Peace with God: The Secret of Happiness* (Nashville: Thomas Nelson, 2000), 202.
5. Kristin Jack, "Jesus Doesn't Want You to Be Happy," Urbana Student Missions Conferences blog, October 11, 2005, http://urbana.org/go-and-do/missional-life /jesus-doesnt-want-you-be-happy.

DAY 14: *Is God Happy?*

1. *Chariots of Fire*, directed by Hugh Hudson (Twentieth Century Fox, 1981).

2. Ibid.
3. Noah Webster, *An American Dictionary of the English Language*, vol. 1 (New York: S. Converse, 1828), 273.

DAY 17: *Does Obeying God Mean Sacrificing Our Happiness?*

1. A Lois Lane, "Experiment 3.3: Why I Cannot Be a Happy Single, Part 1," *The Singleness Experiments* (blog), https://singlenessexperiments.wordpress.com/category /uncategorized/.
2. Charles H. Spurgeon, "Christ's Joy and Ours" (Sermon #2935).

DAY 18: *Why Aren't Christians Known for Their Happiness?*

1. David Kinnaman and Gabe Lyons, *UnChristian: What a New Generation Really Thinks about Christianity . . . and Why It Matters* (Grand Rapids, MI: Baker, 2007), 27.
2. Jonathan Edwards, "Resolutions," *The Works of Jonathan Edwards*, vol. 1, resolution #22.

DAY 19: *Must We Choose between Our Happiness and God's Glory?*

1. Janet Bartholomew, *Does God Care?* (Bloomington, IN: Xlibris Corporation, 2000), 153–54.
2. Charles H. Spurgeon, *The Autobiography of Charles H. Spurgeon: Compiled from His Diary, Letters, and Records*, vol. 1.
3. A. W. Tozer, *Who Put Jesus on the Cross?* (Camp Hill, PA: WingSpread, 2009), e-book.

DAY 20: *If Christians Shouldn't Be Happy, Who Should Be?*

1. H. L. Mencken, *A Mencken Chrestomathy* (New York: Vintage Books, 1982), 624.
2. Thomas Aquinas, *Summa Theologica*, Prima Secundae Partis, question 5, article 4.

DAY 21: *Are Humankind's Desires Sinful?*

1. C. S. Lewis, *The Weight of Glory* (New York: HarperCollins, 2001), 26.
2. Helen H. Lemmel, "Turn Your Eyes upon Jesus," 1922.
3. Jonathan Edwards, "His Early and Rapturous Sense of Divine Things."
4. Peter Kreeft, ed., *A Shorter Summa: The Most Essential Philosophical Passages of St. Thomas Aquinas* (San Francisco: Ignatius Press, 1993), 144.

DAY 22: *What's So Good about the Good News?*

1. Some of my thoughts here are inspired by William Morrice, *Joy in the New Testament* (Grand Rapids, MI: Eerdmans, 1985), 11.
2. Ibid., 12.
3. Ibid.
4. J. Gresham Machen, *What Is Faith?* rev. ed. (Edinburgh: Banner of Truth, 1991), 153.

DAY 23: *Is Seeking Happiness Unspiritual?*

1. Randy Alcorn, *Heaven* (Carol Stream, IL: Tyndale, 2004), 52.

notes

DAY 24: *Is Physical Pleasure Evil?*
1. C. S. Lewis, *Mere Christianity* (New York: HarperCollins, 2001), "Sexual Morality."
2. *Babette's Feast*, directed by Gabriel Axel (Panorama Films, 1987).

DAY 25: *Can the Search for Happiness Become an Idol?*
1. Timothy Keller, *Counterfeit Gods: The Empty Promises of Money, Sex, and Power, and the Only Hope That Matters* (New York: Dutton, 2009), xi–xii.
2. John Piper, "We Want You to Be a Christian Hedonist!" Desiring God, August 31, 2006, http://www.desiringgod.org/ResourceLibrary/Articles/ByDate/2006/1797_We_Want_You.

DAY 26: *How Does Seeing God Accurately Promote Lasting Happiness?*
1. Graham Noble, "The Life and Death of the Terrible Turk," *Eurozine*, May 23, 2003, http://www.eurozine.com/articles/2003-05-23-noble-en.html.
2. "The Stanley Tam Story," YouTube video, 1:01:55, posted by U.S. Plastic Corporation, April 9, 2014, https://www.youtube.com/watch?v=QxPGFlxTSro.
3. Timothy Keller, "Talking about Idolatry in a Postmodern Age," Monergism.com, April 1, 2007, http://www.monergism.com/content/talking-about-idolatry-postmodern-age.

DAY 27: *Who or What Is Our Primary Source of Happiness?*
1. Samuel Rutherford, *Letters of Samuel Rutherford* (Edinburgh: Banner of Truth, 1973), 209.
2. John Gibbon, in James Nichols, Samuel Annesley, eds., *Puritan Sermons, 1659–1689*, repr., vol. 1 (Wheaton, IL: Richard Owen Roberts, 1981), 99.

DAY 28: *How Can Pleasure Point Us to God?*
1. C. S. Lewis, *The Complete C. S. Lewis Signature Classics* (New York: HarperCollins, 2007), 221.
2. Richard L. Bushman, ed., *The Great Awakening: Documents on the Revival of Religion, 1740–1745* (Chapel Hill: University of North Carolina Press, 1989), 30.

DAY 29: *How Can Enjoying Happiness in God's Creation Draw Us to God?*
1. J. R. R. Tolkien, *The Fellowship of the Ring* (New York: Houghton Mifflin, 1966), 339.

DAY 31: *How Does Creation Demonstrate God's Happiness?*
1. DK Publishing, *Off the Tourist Trail: 1,000 Unexpected Travel Alternatives* (London: DK Travel, 2009), 173.
2. A. W. Tozer, *The Attributes of God*, vol. 1 (Camp Hill, PA: WingSpread, 2007), 10, 12–13.
3. "25 Weirdest Looking Animals," *Pagog!* August 11, 2007, http://www.pagog.com/2007/08/11/25-weirdest-looking-animals/.
4. Charles H. Spurgeon, "A Free Salvation" (Sermon #199).

DAY 32: *What Makes Our Father Happy?*

1. Steven M. Studebaker and Robert W. Caldwell III, *The Trinitarian Theology of Jonathan Edwards* (Surrey, UK: Ashgate, 2012), 52.
2. W. Gesenius and S. P. Tregelles, *Gesenius' Hebrew-Chaldee Lexicon to the Old Testament* (Bellingham, WA: Logos Research Systems, 2003).
3. James Swanson, *A Dictionary of Biblical Languages with Semantic Domains: Hebrew (Old Testament)* (Oak Harbor, WA: Logos Research Systems, 1997).
4. *The A. W. Tozer Bible (King James Version)* (Peabody, MA: Hendrickson, 2012), 1086.

DAY 33: *Is Calling God Happy Blasphemous . . . or at Least Disrespectful?*

1. Mack R. Douglas, *How to Make a Habit of Succeeding* (Gretna, LA: Pelican, 1994), 30.
2. Charles H. Spurgeon, "Adorning the Gospel" (Sermon #2416).
3. James A. Wallace, *Preaching to the Hungers of the Heart: The Homily on the Feasts and within the Rites* (Collegeville, MN: Liturgical Press, 2002), 61.

DAY 34: *When Did Happiness Begin?*

1. "A Father's Love: The World's Strongest Dad," YouTube video, 10:00, posted by "Proud to be an Indian," December 3, 2011, https://www.youtube.com/watch?v=ax4VIVs-qsE; "Father Runs Triathlon with His Son in Tow," YouTube video, 4:14, posted by "Truth and Charity," September 20, 2008, https://www.youtube.com/watch?v=UH943Az_lPQ.
2. Michael Reeves, *Delighting in the Trinity* (Downers Grove, IL: InterVarsity Press, 2012), 16.
3. Augustus H. Strong, *Systematic Theology* (Philadelphia: American Baptist Publication Society, 1907), 347.
4. Steve DeWitt, *Eyes Wide Open: Enjoying God in Everything* (Grand Rapids, MI: Credo House, 2012), 46–47.

DAY 36: *Is God's Happiness Confined to Heaven?*

1. Charles H. Spurgeon, "Israel's God and God's Israel" (Sermon #803).
2. Spurgeon, "Joy and Peace in Believing" (Sermon #692).
3. Norman Cousins, *Anatomy of an Illness* (New York: W. W. Norton, 1979).
4. Jonathan Edwards, in John Piper, "Undoing the Destruction of Pleasure," Desiring God, April 10, 2001, http://www.desiringgod.org/conference-messages/undoing-the-destruction-of-pleasure.
5. Victor Hugo, *Les Misérables*, chapter 4.
6. John Bunyan, "Christ: A Complete Saviour," *The Works of John Bunyan*, vol. 1.

DAY 37: *Is God's Happiness a New Thought?*

1. Arthur Hyman, James J. Walsh, and Thomas Williams, eds., *Philosophy in the Middle Ages* (Indianapolis: Hackett, 2010), 158.
2. Matthew Henry, *Matthew Henry's Commentary on the Whole Bible*, vol. 1, Genesis 2:1-3.
3. John Gill, "Of the Blessedness of God," *A Body of Doctrinal Divinity*, book 1.

notes

4. H. D. M. Spence-Jones, ed., *The Pulpit Commentary: Jeremiah*, vol. 2.
5. John McReynolds, "The Happiness of God," Global Jesus Christ Network, August 17, 2010, http://www.gjcn.org/2010/08/basics-15-the-happiness-of-god/.

DAY 38: *Why Were So Many People Attracted to Jesus?*

1. Sherwood E. Wirt, *Jesus, Man of Joy* (Eugene, OR: Harvest House, 1999), 10–11.
2. "Amanda's Reason to Remember," About.com, http://christianity.about.com/od /miraculousintervention/a/amandatestimony.htm.
3. A. W. Tozer, *The Pursuit of God* (Ventura, CA: Regal, 2013), 40.
4. E. Stanley Jones, "We Turn to Our Resources," *Abundant Living: 364 Daily Devotions* (Nashville: Abingdon Press, 2014).

DAY 39: *Is Jesus Happy?*

1. Dylan Demarsico, "In the Beginning Was Laughter," *The Behemoth*, Christianity Today, September 18, 2014, http://www.christianitytoday.com/behemoth/2014/issue -5/in-beginning-was-laughter.html.
2. Ibid.
3. John Piper, *Seeing and Savoring Jesus Christ* (Wheaton, IL: Crossway, 2004), 36.

DAY 41: *Can Happiness Really Be Spiritual?*

1. Isaac Watts, *The Psalms and Hymns of Isaac Watts* (Oak Harbor, WA: Logos Research Systems, Inc., 1998).
2. Charles H. Spurgeon, "Christ's Joy and Ours" (Sermon #2935).
3. A. W. Tozer, *Life in the Spirit* (Peabody, MA: Hendrickson, 2009), 153.
4. Mike Mason, *Champagne for the Soul: Celebrating God's Gift of Joy* (Vancouver, BC: Regent College, 2003), 31.
5. David Murray, "7 Kinds of Happiness," *HeadHeartHand* (blog), September 17, 2014, http://headhearthand.org/blog/2014/09/17/7-types-of-happiness/.
6. Charles H. Spurgeon, *The Treasury of David*, Psalm 150.

DAY 42: *What Role Do Our Attitudes Play in Our Happiness?*

1. Epictetus, *Enchiridion* (New York: Dover, 2004), 3.
2. Helen Keller, as quoted in Amy E. Dean, *Peace of Mind: Daily Meditations for Easing Stress* (New York: Bantam, 1995), 364.
3. David Brainerd, as quoted in Jonathan Edwards, *Life and Diary of David Brainerd* (New York: Cosimo, 2007), 78–79.
4. Ibid., 81.
5. Ibid., 90.
6. Ibid., 112.
7. Ibid., 151.
8. Ibid., 153, 183.
9. David Brainerd, as quoted in Jonathan Edwards, *The Life of the Rev. David Brainerd, Missionary to the Indians* (Edinburgh: H. S. Baynes, 1824), 302.

DAY 43: *How Do Our Actions Affect Our Happiness?*

1. Sonja Lyubomirsky, *The How of Happiness: A Scientific Approach to Getting the Life You Want* (New York: Penguin Books, 2007), 20–21.

2. Ibid., 20–23.

3. Therese J. Borchard, "How Giving Makes Us Happy," *World of Psychology* (blog), PsychCentral.com, December 22, 2013, http://psychcentral.com/blog/archives/2013/12/22/how-giving-makes-us-happy/.

DAY 45: *What Can We Do to Cultivate Happiness?*

1. Cathy Miller, "Delayed Delivery," as quoted in Joe Wheeler, *The Best of Christmas in My Heart*, vol. 2 (Brentwood, TN: Howard, 2008).

2. Martin E. P. Seligman, *Learned Optimism* (New York: Knopf, 1991), 4–5.

3. Dennis Prager, *Happiness Is a Serious Problem: A Human Nature Repair Manual* (New York: ReganBooks, 1998), 24.

DAY 46: *What Choice Do We Have When It Comes to Happiness?*

1. Randy Alcorn, *The Purity Principle* (Sisters, OR: Multnomah, 2003), 9–10.

DAY 47: *Why Should We Care about Making Others Happy?*

1. Lou Nicholes, *Romans: A Roadmap for the Christian Life* (Fairfax, VA: Xulon Press, 2004), 113.

2. Bernard Rimland, "The Altruism Paradox," *Psychological Reports* 51, no. 2 (October 1982): 521–22, http://prx.sagepub.com/content/51/2/521.full.pdf+html.

3. Ibid.

4. Arthur C. Brooks, as quoted in "Those Who Serve Others Are *Happier, Healthier*, and More *Prosperous*," Spokane Cares, http://www.spokanecares.org/index.php?c_ref=160.

DAY 48: *Can Feasts and Celebrations Please God?*

1. Warren Wiersbe, *The Wycliffe Handbook of Preaching and Preachers* (Chicago: Moody Press, 1984), 187.

2. William G. Morrice, *We Joy in God* (London: SPCK, 1977), 52.

3. Charles H. Spurgeon, "To Those Who Feel Unfit for Communion" (Sermon #2131).

DAY 49: *How Can Reading God's Word Promote Lasting Happiness?*

1. Arthur T. Pierson, *George Müller of Bristol (1805–1898)* (Peabody, MA: Hendrickson, 2008), 130–31.

2. George Müller, "How to Be Happy and Strong in the Lord," in *Guide to Holiness*, vol. 18–19 (New York: Walter C. Palmer, 1871), 78.

3. George Müller, "Joyfulness and Usefulness," in *The Advocate of Christian Holiness* (January, 1880), 7.

4. Calvin Miller, *The Taste of Joy: Recovering the Lost Glow of Discipleship* (Downers Grove, IL: InterVarsity Press, 1983), 18.

5. Charles H. Spurgeon, "Repentance after Conversion" (Sermon #2419).

notes

DAY 51: *How Does Forgiveness Relate to Our Happiness?*

1. Ruth Bell Graham, *Legacy of a Pack Rat* (Nashville: Thomas Nelson, 1989), 187.
2. Charles H. Spurgeon, "Sorrow and Sorrow" (Sermon #2691).
3. Martin Luther, "Sermon for the 19th Sunday after Trinity," *Sermons of Martin Luther*.

DAY 52: *Must We Choose between Holiness and Happiness?*

1. Richard Mansel, "God Calls Us to Holiness, Not Happiness," *Forthright Magazine*, March 4, 2008, http://forthright.net/2008/03/04/god_calls_us_to_holiness_not _happiness_1/.
2. Tony Reinke, "The World's Joy-Tragedy," Desiring God, August 30, 2014, http://www .desiringgod.org/articles/the-world-s-joy-tragedy.
3. Mark David Futato, *Interpreting the Psalms: An Exegetical Handbook* (Grand Rapids, MI: Kregel, 2007), 67.

DAY 53: *Is Seeking Happiness Selfish?*

1. C. S. Lewis, *The Weight of Glory* (New York: HarperCollins, 2001), 25.
2. Ibid., 25–26.

DAY 54: *Can Self-Forgetfulness Make Us Happier?*

1. C. S. Lewis, *Mere Christianity* (New York: HarperCollins, 2001), book 3, chapter 8, "The Great Sin."
2. Tom Robbins, *Jitterbug Perfume* (New York: Bantam, 2003), 261.
3. Timothy Keller, *The Freedom of Self-Forgetfulness* (Denver: 10Publishing, 2012), 32–33.

DAY 55: *What Does Thankfulness Have to Do with Happiness?*

1. Matthew Henry, quoted in James S. Hewett, ed., *Illustrations Unlimited* (Carol Stream, IL: Tyndale, 1988), 264.

DAY 56: *Do We Have a Right to Expect Happiness in a World of Worry?*

1. Morley Safer, "The Pursuit of Happiness," CBS News video, 12:06, from *60 Minutes*, June 15, 2008, http://www.cbsnews.com/video/watch/?id=4181996n.
2. Max Lucado, *And the Angels Were Silent* (Nashville: Thomas Nelson, 2013), 105–6.

DAY 57: *What Does God Promise Us about Eternal Happiness?*

1. Seneca, as quoted by David G. Myers, *Psychology*, 6th ed. (New York: Worth, 2001), 484.
2. A. W. Tozer and H. Verploegh, *The Quotable Tozer II: More Wise Words with a Prophetic Edge* (Camp Hill, PA: Christian Publications, 1997), 103.
3. Richard Baxter and William Orme, "The Divine Life: Walking with God," *The Practical Works of the Rev. Richard Baxter*, vol. 13.

DAY 58: *What Happiness Can We Anticipate on the New Earth?*

1. *The Lord of the Rings: The Return of the King*, directed by Peter Jackson (New Line Cinema, 2003).

DAY 59: *Is Unending Happiness Too Good to Be True?*

1. C. S. Lewis, *Mere Christianity* (New York: HarperCollins, 2001), book 4, chapter 4, "Good Infection."
2. Brother Lawrence and Frank Laubach, *Practicing His Presence* (Sargent, GA: The SeedSowers, 1973), 10.
3. Ibid.
4. John Piper, *Don't Waste Your Life* (Wheaton, IL: Crossway, 2003), 10.

DAY 60: *Will We Really Live Happily Ever After?*

1. John H. Sammis, "Trust and Obey," *Church Hymnal* (Cleveland, TN: Tennessee Music and Printing, 1951), 157.
2. John Calvin, *Commentary on the Book of Psalms*, vol. 2, Psalm 37:27-29.
3. Charles H. Spurgeon, "A Message to the Glad and the Sad" (Sermon #2546).

ABOUT THE
Author

RANDY ALCORN is an author and the founder and director of Eternal Perspective Ministries (EPM), a nonprofit organization dedicated to teaching principles of God's Word and assisting the church in ministering to unreached, unfed, unborn, uneducated, unreconciled, and unsupported people around the world. His ministry focus is communicating the strategic importance of using our earthly time, money, possessions, and opportunities to invest in need-meeting ministries that count for eternity. He accomplishes this by analyzing, teaching, and applying biblical truth.

Before starting EPM in 1990, Randy served as a pastor for fourteen years. He has a bachelor of theology and a master of arts in biblical studies from Multnomah University and an honorary doctorate from Western Seminary in Portland, Oregon, and has taught on the adjunct faculties of both. A *New York Times* bestselling author, Randy has written more than fifty books, including *Heaven*, *The Treasure Principle*, and the award-winning novel *Safely Home*. Sales of his books are about ten million copies and have been translated into more than sixty languages. Randy has written for many magazines, including EPM's *Eternal Perspectives*. He is active on Facebook and Twitter and has been a guest on more than eight hundred radio, television, and online programs, including *Focus on the Family*, *FamilyLife Today*, *Revive Our Hearts*, and *Bible Answer Man*.

Randy resides in Gresham, Oregon, with his wife, Nanci. They have two married daughters and are the proud grandparents of five grandsons. Randy enjoys time spent with his family, biking, underwater photography, research, and reading.

You may contact Eternal Perspective Ministries at www.epm.org or 39085 Pioneer Blvd., Suite 206, Sandy, OR 97055 or 503-668-5200. Follow Randy on Facebook: www.facebook.com/randyalcorn, on Twitter: www.twitter.com/randyalcorn, and on his blog: www.epm.org/blog.

Think God doesn't want
you to be happy?

Think again.

Join noted theologian Randy Alcorn as he shows us
how we can experience all the happiness God has
to offer in *Happiness*, *God's Promise of Happiness*,
and *60 Days of Happiness*. These books will forever
change the way you think about happiness.